# Mary's Ankle ..

# MARY'S ANKLE

## *A FARCICAL DISPLAY IN THREE VIEWS*

BY

MAY TULLY

SAMUEL FRENCH, INC.
25 WEST 45TH STREET, NEW YORK, N. Y.
811 WEST 7TH STREET, LOS ANGELES, CALIF.
SAMUEL FRENCH, LTD.
26 SOUTHAMPTON STREET, STRAND, W.C.2, LONDON

"MARY'S ANKLE"



Especial notice should be taken that the possession of this book without a valid contract for production first having been obtained from the publisher confers no right or license to professionals or amateurs to produce the play publicly or in private for gain or charity.

In its present form this play is dedicated to the reading public only, and no performance, representation, production, recitation, public reading or radio broadcasting may be given except by special arrangement with Samuel French, at 25 West 45th Street, New York City, or at 811 West 7th Street, Los Angeles, Calif.

This play may be presented by amateurs upon payment of a royalty of Twenty-Five Dollars for each performance, payable to Samuel French, at 25 West 45th Street, New York, or at 811 West 7th Street, Los Angeles, Calif., one week before the date when the play is given.

Whenever the play is produced the following notice must appear on all programs, printing and advertising for the play: "Produced by special arrangement with Samuel French."

Attention is called to the penalty provided by law for any infringement of the author's rights, as follows:

"Section 4966:—Any person publicly performing or representing any dramatic or musical composition for which copyright has been obtained, without the consent of the proprietor of said dramatic or musical composition, or his heirs and assigns, shall be liable for damages thereof, such damages in all cases to be assessed at such sum, not less than one hundred dollars for the first and fifty dollars for every subsequent performance, as to the court shall appear to be just. If the unlawful performance and representation be wilful and for profit, such person or persons shall be guilty of a misdemeanor, and upon conviction shall be imprisoned for a period not exceeding one year."—U. S. Revised Statutes: Title 60, Chap. 3.

Copy of original program of "MARY'S ANKLE," as produced at the Bijou Theatre, New York:

A. H. WOODS
(In association with Rosalie Stewart and May Tully)

Presents

"MARY'S ANKLE"

*A Farcical Display in Three Views*

*By* MAY TULLY

CAST

DOCTOR HAMPTON (DOC) .............. *Bert Lytell*
G. P. HAMPTON (G. P.).............. *Walter Jones*
STOKES ............................ *T. W. Gibson*
CHUB ............................. *Leo Donnelly*
MARY JANE SMITH ................. *Irene Fenwick*
CLEMENTINE (CLEM) .............. *Louise Drew*
MRS. BURNS .................... *Adelaide Prince*
MRS. MERRIVALE ................... *Zelda Sears*
STEWARD .......................... *Barnet Parker*
EXPRESSMAN ................... *Wm. J. Morrisey*

SYNOPSIS OF SCENES

ACT I. *The combined office and living room of* DR.
HAMPTON *in* MRS. MERRIVALE'S *house
in New York City.*

ACT II. *The same. Ten days later.*

ACT III. *Deck of the Steamship Bermudian. One hour
later.*

TIME: *The present.*

# THE CHARACTERS

DOCTOR HAMPTON—"DOC": *A most attractive and enthusiastic young chap, who has just completed his required interneship in one of the larger city hospitals and set up an office of his own. He is surrounded by loving friends but, as yet, no patients. His magnetic personality, however, plus his great charm of manner, his quality of never being too down to bounce, his interest in and sweetness to everybody with whom he comes in contact, mark him instantly as one of the few born to be successful. So it is merely a matter of watchful waiting for that first patient—that first patient so necessary to the building up of a doctor's large and profitable practice.*

STOKES—"STOKSIE": *One of "Doc" Hampton's loving friends, who has chosen the Law as his means of providing himself with daily bread and butter, but who is now beginning to doubt the wisdom of his choice because of the fact that no one is showing any signs of needing his legal services and the very thought of going out after clients and business is more than his quiet, studious soul can bear. He is at his best behind a pipe, book or desk.*

"CHUB": *Another of "Doc" Hampton's loving friends, whose tongue keeps pace with his thoughts but who, for all his chatter, is sincere. He verges on the fresh but is never in any way obnoxious. His ambition is to make a name and fortune for himself.*

4

# DESCRIPTION OF CHARACTERS

CLEMENTINE: *Mrs. Merrivale's common, calculating, shrill-voiced and acid-tongued daughter, who, with all her faults, is absolutely honest and without affectation. Her mother, with her fancied invalidism, is the proverbial red rag to her and is only tolerated by her as the easiest way out of a difficult family situation.*

MRS. MERRIVALE: *"Doc" Hampton's landlady, who has made his maintaining an office in her house, without so much as a sign of a patient, a possibility because of her weakness for doctors' services and her constant enjoyment of poor health. Although she has never known a day's real illness in her life, she has turned herself into a hypochondriac to avoid housework and to obtain for herself the most attention for the least exertion. She has ever labored under the delusion that she is cultured and attractive, while dressing and looking the part of a coquette.*

MARY JANE SMITH: *"Doc" Hampton's first patient, due to the fact that her car crashed just outside his door. She is the Junior League girl of today—expensively simple in dress, with that priceless well-bred assurance resulting from always having and doing the best with the best. Romantic and susceptible, she succumbs to "Doc's" magnetic personality, inwardly, while, outwardly, her sense of humor keeps them all guessing.*

MRS. BURNS: *Mary's Aunt, who is a charming, beautifully gowned lady with all the social graces of one to the manor born, and possessing, in addition, a delightful sense of humor. For all her apparent outward femininity and softness she can be rock firm when, in her opinion, occasion demands.*

G. P. HAMPTON: *"Doc" Hampton's uncle, who is a vital, blustering, gruff, but perfectly harmless, business man with a hearty laugh and a stacatto manner of clipping off his words, which add importance to himself and what he says. His pleasure is in controlling situations and people, and he has managed successfully to keep his young nephew in awe of him by holding the strings of his money-bags in a rather tight fist and assuming a forbidding facial expression. In reality, he is quite lenient, most generous, and exceedingly pleasant.*

THE STEWARD: *Who is always on deck with his constant and annoying subservient intrusions, whether wanted or not. He has an unconsciously humorous rhythmic walk which suggests effeminacy, but not distastefully, and an uncontrollable little break in his voice when he is most intense which invariably brings on an embarrassed nervous giggle that will only cease when he gulps abruptly. He is the only one attaching any importance to himself.*

# MARY'S ANKLE

## ACT ONE

SCENE: *Combined office and living room of Dr. Hampton.*

*It is a front parlor of a furnished-room house in the Sixties between Lexington and Third Avenues, New York. Dr. Hampton has but recently graduated from college. His room is furnished in R. side as an office and on the L. as a living room. There is a couch on which he sleeps, a desk, table with instruments, practical wash-basin, cabinet, doctor's screen, dressing-table, bookcase, some easy chairs, etc. There is a door up L. to street; door R.C. to bathroom; windows down R. and L. The blinds are down and LIGHTS ¼ up.*

AS CURTAIN RISES: STOKES *is discovered wrapped in blanket on Doctor's operating or examining chair. His shoes are Left of chair.* DOCTOR *is asleep on couch. After a moment there is a* KNOCK *on the L. door. This is repeated several times until the* DOCTOR *awakens and hastily slips on bathrobe and slippers. He moves cautiously to door and stands with ear to crack, listening.*

7

Doc. *(Softly)* Who is it?

Chub. *(Off stage)* It's Chub—let me in.

Doc. *(Turns key in door but doesn't bother opening it. Falls back on couch as* Chub *enters)* You have your nerve waking people up in the middle of the night.

Chub. *(Has newspaper in his hand. It is opened at the financial page)* Middle of the night? Why, the day's almost over!

Doc. What time is it? *(Half rising.)*

Chub. *(Raises blind* L. *LIGHTS ½ up)* Ten o'clock—your office hours. Get up and be ready for business. How do you expect to get along if you sleep all day?

Doc. *(Leaning elbow on pillow)* Dry up.

Chub. *(During this* Chub *pulls up blind, letting in a flood of sunlight. LIGHTS now full up. It blinds* Doc *on the couch and disturbs* Stokes, *who moves uneasily on chair)* Remember the story of the Wise Virgin who kept her lamp trimmed.

Doc. Yes, but I'm no Virgin—and I have no lamp. *(Yawns.* Stokes *has lain as still as a dead man, sheet up over his head. He suddenly hears noise and sits up, pulling off sheet.)*

Chub. *(Sees* Stokes*)* Doc, what the deuce—— Who——

Stokes. *(Stirs in chair and finally wakes)* What's the row?

Chub. *(Crossing to* R.*)* Look who's here! I didn't notice you, Stoksie. *(Breaks operating chair, spilling* Stokes *on the floor.)*

Stokes. That's nothing, Chub—I don't even notice myself lately.

Chub. *(Sees chafing-dish and three empty beer bottles on* Doc's *desk)* Ah—ha! No wonder you two couldn't get up after carousing all night. Look at this. Three bottles of beer and a welsh rarebit—that must have cost a couple of dollars. *(With a very superior air)* And still you fellows wonder why you don't succeed! *(There is a KNOCK at the door L. Doc jumps up.)*

Doc. Who is it?

Clem. *(Off stage)* Can I fix your room up now?

Doc. Yes—just a minute.

Clem. It's after ten.

Doc. Get into the bathroom, Stoksie. I don't want her to know that you were here last night. Chub, sit over there and be a patient. *(During above Clem ad libs. off stage—"Let me come in. I can't wait all day. Have other work to do." Doc pushing beer bottles in doctor's medical case and chafing-dish in the bottom drawer of desk, also throws comforter and pillow from examining-chair to the couch)* Come in.

Clem. *(Enters with carpet-sweeper and towels and duster)* I knocked twict before but nobody answered.

Doc. I was up quite late last night on an urgent case.

Clem. *(Suspiciously)* Case of what? *(Chub has difficulty in suppressing laugh. He is sitting on R. window ledge. Stokes is in bathroom, dressing.)*

Doc. You'll pardon my being dressed like this.

Clem. Yes—it is kinda loud, ain't it? *(She walks to washbasin. As she passes desk she sniffs audibly)* What a funny smell.

Doc. *(Realizing she smells cheese in the chafing-dish)* Yes—it's a medicinal odor.

Clem. It smells cheesy to me. *(Puts Doctor's grip on the floor. Doc takes the towels. There is a rattle of bottles inside grip as she does so)* Medicinal bottles, I suppose?

Doc. Yes.

Clem. I know your office hours are supposed to be from ten to four, and as I ain't never seen no crowd waiting at ten, I thought if I was a few minutes late it wouldn't hurt. *(Crosses to couch. CHUB has been trying to keep silent but coughs aloud at this. Doc gathers his clothes, preparing to go to bathroom to dress)* My Gawd! He has got a patient! *(Her attitude changes entirely)* I won't be a minute, sir. *(She folds up bedclothes hurriedly and puts them in the closet c. during the ensuing scene.)*

Doc. *(To CHUB)* You'll excuse me while I dress. *(Goes into bathroom.)*

CHUB. Certainly, Doctor.

CLEM. I had no idea there was a patient waiting.

CHUB. That's quite all right, I'm sure.

CLEM. I'll just fix up the bed and I'll come back later and clean out the room. I was only joking with the Doctor just now when I said I ain't seen no patients here. Maybe he has some but *I* ain't seen any—that's all.

CHUB. Oh, you surprise me.

CLEM. *(Very confidentially)* But don't let that interfere with you. Goodness knows I don't want to be the cause of his losing a patient. We've rent this front parlor to a doctor ever since we've had this house, and there ain't none of them ever been any good, to my way of thinkin'. *(Still lower voice)* He's too young to suit me.

CHUB. But all doctors must begin some time.

CLEM. *(Starts up c.)* Sure—but they don't have to begin on me. I ain't knocking him, only I wish Maw would rent the parlor to someone who'd pay. *(Takes sheets and spread to closet. STOKES sneaks out for his shoes and is almost seen by CLEM. Door of bathroom partly open and Doc and STOKES are seen from here on.)*

CHUB. Do you mean to say that Doctor Hampton doesn't pay his rent?

CLEM. *(Back to couch)* He never gets a chance in this house. You know, Maw thinks she is an invalid. There ain't a disease in the world she ain't had—or hopes to have. She swears by Dr. Hampton. He treats her and she lets him have this room *rent free. (Takes pillows to closet.)*

CHUB. Oh—ho! That's it, is it?

CLEM. That's what?

CHUB. *(Catching himself)* That's what he *does.*

CLEM. Yes, that's what he does. It suits Maw and it suits Dr. Hampton, I guess. The only person it don't suit is me.

CHUB. No?

CLEM. No—— *(Slams closet door. Comes to couch with sofa-pillows)* As long as there's a doctor in the house Maw thinks she's sick, and as long as Maw thinks she's sick I have to do all the work. That's why I'm down on the medical profession. *(Hits pillow. STOKES appears from bathroom, laughing silently. Doc reaches out violently and pulls him back. CLEM keeps on talking)* However, there ain't no use kicking. *(Gathers up her things)* Goodbye. *(She exits L. CHUB falls on couch, laughing. STOKES comes from bathroom, dressed. He is also convulsed with laughter. Doc follows, partly dressed.)*

CHUB. Now I know your secret, Doc. Now I know how you manage to stay in one house so long while Stoksie and I have been hopping from one hall bedroom to another like a couple of mountain goats. *(STOKES laughs. Doc goes to bathroom to finish dressing.)* Say, by the way, boys, Steel has gone up to a hundred and thirty.

STOKES. *(Sarcastically)* You don't say.

CHUB. Remember I gave you a tip on that when it was selling at seventy-two.

STOKES. *(With mock seriousness)* You did?

CHUB. Do you know what you would have made if you had followed by tip? A thousand dollars invested at seventy-two—it's now a hundred and thirty—that would be fifty-eight thousand dollars' profit. Think of that—fifty-eight thousand dollars!

STOKES. I can't think of it. There's only one trouble with that tip, Chub.

CHUB. What is that?

STOKES. You didn't tip me off how to get the thousand.

CHUB. Oh—of course——

STOKES. Now, what's the use of raving this way, Chub? You're broke, Doc's riding on a flat tire, and I rattle like a set of bones in a minstrel show, and yet you come here day after day and tell us how to clean up Wall Street.

DOC. What's he doing, Stokes? *(Comes fully dressed from bathroom)* Telling you how much money you could make if you could make some money? How is it with you, Chub—you seemed in good spirits when you first came in?

CHUB. *(Crossing to desk)* Well—nothing definite, but I have a couple of good things in view. *(STOKES goes to window, sits on R. window-sill and looks out. Doc sits R. of desk.)*

DOC. The point is, Chub, have you any money?

CHUB. Well, I'll tell you! I have——

DOC. That's enough. Go no further.

CHUB. I was wondering if I could make a touch.

DOC. Oh, ho! Wait a minute. Did you hear that, Stokes?

STOKES. No—what was it?

DOC. Chub here wants to borrow some money.

STOKES. Well, I'm in favor of that. From whom?

DOC. From us. *(Doc and STOKES both give CHUB the laugh. STOKES crosses to chair L. of desk.)*

CHUB. What's the joke?

DOC. *You* are, Chub. *You* are.

CHUB. *(Comes behind desk)* Well, I haven't seen

you for two or three days. I thought you might have one patient by now, anyway.

Doc. I haven't had one patient since I opened my office.

Chub. How's the Law, Stokes? (Stokes *grunts disgustedly.*) I see. *(Attempting to be cheerful)* Oh, come on, fellows, cheer up. Of course we must all begin at the bottom.

Stokes. That's all I hear—"begin at the bottom" —"begin at the bottom"—— Well, I'm at the bottom, all right, but I can't begin.

Doc. You know what I think, fellows——

Both. What?

Doc. I think somebody put a curse on the three of us.

Both. You do, Doc?

Doc. There's a Jonah somewhere, that's certain. *(There is a pause as they look dejected. Doc tries to whistle as he arranges his desk; but fails miserably. He picks up appointment pad and runs finger on pages. It is absolutely blank.)*

Chub. It's *funny* we can't get started, isn't it?

Doc. It's a scream.

Chub. How do you account for it?

Doc. It's the business. The medical profession is overcrowded. It's a rotten business, anyway. Now, if I had gone in for Law like Stokes.

Stokes. Law! Law! You poor, deluded quack. A *lawyer* has no chance at all.

Doc. It's better than Medicine.

Stokes. It is not!

Doc. Anybody who says Medicine is better than Law ought to have his head examined.

Stokes. Yes, by a doctor. You see—there's some trade for him right there.

Doc. *(Angry, rising)* Are you trying to tell me I made a good choice when I took up Medicine?

Stokes. You made a better choice than I did

*(Rises also. ALL in the same positions at desk. Doc and STOKES are shouting.)*

Doc. What? If you're a lawyer—well—you can argue someone into a lawsuit, but by golly you can't argue them into being sick.

STOKES. But people get sick when they can't help it—and they're liable to stumble on to any old doctor—even you, for instance.

Doc. What do you mean, even me? Didn't I graduate with honors? That's more than you did.

CHUB. *(Trying to calm them)* Gentlemen—gentlemen—let me pour oil on the troubled waters.

Doc. I don't want any oil. When a fellow tells me Medicine is a regular business I want to fight.

STOKES. Well—they're *both* rotten businesses! *(Crossing L. CHUB is still upstage behind desk.)*

Doc. All right—they're both rotten—but medicine is the rottenest of all! I wouldn't mind if I could just make a living, but what am I going to do? A doctor can't go out and hustle business—it's considered unethical.

CHUB. Of course you couldn't do that.

Doc. Although I don't see why not. I don't see why I shouldn't have as much right as an insurance agent to walk into a man's office and try and interest him in me.

CHUB. That's silly! What would you say? "Pardon me, but could I interest you in some nice new diseases this morning?"

Doc. No—but I could tell him how good a doctor I am, couldn't I?

STOKES. Not truthfully.

Doc. But if I did, that's just the time he would avoid me when he was sick—he'd think I was a quack. It's all wrong. *(There is a pause. CHUB and STOKES walk disconsolately upstage.)* I've written my uncle in Fargo, asking him for a loan.

BOTH. *(Turning quickly and eagerly)* Yes?

Doc. Yes. But he hasn't answered yet.

Chub. *(Pulling out lining of his pocket. Broke)* Gee! It was never as bad as this before, was it?

Doc. I didn't think a fellow could be as broke as this and live.

Stokes. Well, he can't live long, that's a cinch. Gee! it looks like back to Decatur for mine. Gosh! I hate to think of it. Did you ever live in one of those small towns?

Chub. You can't tell—they might elect you to Congress.

Doc. You wouldn't want to see that happen to him, would you?

Stokes. I figure a man is as big as his surroundings. I've made my brag about succeeding in New York, so I—I just can't admit I'm licked. *(Sits on couch in reclining position.)*

Chub. You're not licked. None of us is licked.

Doc. Aren't we?

Chub. Certainly not! Some day we will all be famous and we'll look back at this and laugh. *(Sits L. of desk.)*

Doc. *(Sitting R. of desk)* I won't laugh. No doubt I'll be famous and I may look back at this— but I won't have the heart to laugh. *(They pause and sit brooding.)*

Chub. It was all so different when we were at college together. Remember how ambitious we were and how rosy the future looked? *(Stokes buries his head in pillows on couch. They ALL sigh.)*

Doc. Yes—I used to think once I hung out my shingle with "G. Hampton, M.D." they'd have to call out the reserves to keep back the crowd.

Chub. You know what the trouble is?

Doc. No, do you?

Chub. Sure.

Stokes. *(Sitting up on couch)* Well, if you do, why didn't you speak up before?

CHUB. All businesses are rotten until you *succeed.* The point is how to succeed.

STOKES. Now it's coming!

CHUB. To be successful—one must only do the unusual. Success is merely a condition of mind. Stick to the crowd, follow the beaten paths and the supreme ultimate will be mediocrity; but strike out fearlessly, do the unusual, and success is as certain to follow as daylight follows night. *(Rises. As* CHUB *gets into his subject he begins to walk up and down in an important manner)* You know what Shakespeare says—"There is nothing either good or bad but thinking makes it so." That applies to success as well.

DOC. What has been interfering with your thinking all these months?

CHUB. *(Ignoring* DOC*)* Thoughts are things. The thing is to *think* success. Now I'm full of ideas and I know nothing can hold me back.

STOKES. Have you any idea on how to eat when you're broke, Chub?

DOC. I suppose if we three thought we had breakfast now—it would be just as good as if we really had it?

CHUB. It really would—if we really thought it.

STOKES. *(Placing hands to pit of his stomach)* But you don't think we really have had breakfast, do you, Chub?

DOC. Sure he does. He'll be complaining of indigestion next.

CHUB. That's right, make fun of me when I'm trying to tell you something worth while. Of course I don't mean that if you kidded yourself and said, "I've had my breakfast," "I've had my breakfast," and didn't really believe it, that you'd satisfy your hunger, but if you genuinely believed it—*believed* it, understand, you'd be all right.

STOKES. *(Rising from couch)* Get the chloroform, Doc. Here we are, the three of us, broke, no breakfast, and this, *this*—*(Pointing to* CHUB*)* —tells us all we have to do to be successful is to be unusual. Think success! *(Derisively.)*

DOC. *(Jumping about foolishly. As he says his last "success" he grabs a paper knife and goes for* CHUB*)* Yes! Success! Success! Success! Chub, I've thought of a great job for you—something unusual and bound to succeed.

CHUB. What's that?

DOC. Amusement director of an insane asylum. You'd have all the nuts laugh themselves to death at your ideas.

CHUB. *(Very much hurt)* It's no use trying to tell you fellows anything. You are both bromidic— you have no imagination. You make me sick. *(There's a KNOCK on the door.)*

DOC. Come in.

CLEM. *(Enters* L.*)* Maw wants to know if she can come up and see you now?

DOC. *(Going to desk and looking through his list of appointments)* Let me see—— *(In professional tones)* Yes—I think I can squeeze her in all right.

CLEM. Squeeze her in? I hope you ain't reflectin' on Maw's size, Doctor Hampton. *(Exits* L.*)*

DOC. Hurrah! I'm safe in this room another week. The landlady's sick. The landlady's sick. *(Boys take hands and dance around* C.*)*

CLEM. *(Opening door and catches them jumping about. Doc pretends to be examining* CHUB's *throat and ad libs. "Say, Ah.")* Ha—hem—hm—here's some letters I forgot.

STOKES. Letters?

DOC. Ha—ha—some letters? *(Taking letters.)*

CLEM. Bills mostly. *(As she looks them over she exits.)*

STOKES. *(Sits on couch)* Nothing escapes that bird.

Doc. *(Opening mail)* Humn—"Unless payment is made on operating-chair before the fifteenth we will be compelled to take action."

Chub. Looks like you're going to lose your virtuous couch, Stoksie.

Doc. Bills for instruments, furniture—— Hello, here's one from Fargo—my Uncle G. P. *(He opens letters as* Stokes *and* Chub *gather tensely about him. They are standing in* c. *of stage.)* This is the answer to my letter and it's our last chance. *(Shakes envelope for possible check. Nothing falls out. He reads letter)* "My dear Nephew:" Sounds encouraging. *(He repeats)* "My dear Nephew—"

Chub. Sure, when it's a turn-down they usually start off with "Sir—"

Doc. *(Reading)* "I'm sorry I must refuse your request for a loan." *(Glances at* Chub *and* Stokes.)

Chub. Well, his rhetoric is admirable—very concise and to the point.

Doc. *(Reading)* "I realize a young man, just starting in, should have all the latest tools for his trade."

Stokes. He must think you're a brick-layer, Doc.

Doc. *(Reading)* "But I might as well make my position clear and definite once and for all. Your dear father was a dreamer. He and I started out in life with nothing but prospects. Your Dad finished up just the way he started. I needn't tell you that I have been fairly successful, but I made my career carefully and sensibly. I had no one to make the way easy for me—no place to go when I needed help—so I had to help myself or go under. I didn't go under. I don't believe in college education. It's mostly a waste of time. Education is experience and experience is best learned when it is learned first hand. Now you have got your college education, show me, Son, show me. Your loving Uncle,

G. P. Hampton." "Loving Uncle." Can you beat
that? *(Crosses R.)*

CHUB. *(Trying to be cheerful)* Well, Doc—
maybe he's right. Some day you may refer to that
letter as the turning point of your career. (Doc
*and* STOKES *turn on him as if to strangle him.*)

DOC. Oh, Chub!

STOKES. *(Grabbing* CHUB *by the neck)* Shall I
strangle him, Doc, or do you reserve that pleasure?

CHUB. You wait—everything turns out for the
best.

DOC. *(Crushing letter and throwing it on desk)*
Can you beat that old skinflint?

STOKES. Why, he's a multi-millionaire, too, isn't
he?

DOC. I should say he is—a thousand dollars to
him is no more than ten cents to you.

STOKES. *(R. of desk)* Then he is no millionaire,
Doc.

CHUB. *(Crossing to desk)* Say—you know what
you could do if you had that thousand, don't you?
A thousand dollars invested in Steel six months ago
would mean sixty thousand today.

DOC. Honestly?

CHUB. That would be twenty thousand apiece.

DOC. What do you mean twenty thousand apiece?
Do you think I'm going to give you twenty thousand dollars of my money?—I should say not!
(Doc *and* CHUB *are facing each other down stage
over desk.*)

CHUB. You wouldn't? Why, you're worse than
your uncle. You haven't even got the money and
still you won't split it!

DOC. I wouldn't see you want, Chub, and I'd
stake you to a little, but split my sixty thousand
dollars three ways—you ask too much!

STOKES. But Doc, as you haven't the sixty thousand dollars—you might as well let Chub and me have our twenty—don't you think?

Doc. *(Walks up stage around desk)* No, I'm blamed if I will.

Chub. *(To Stokes)* You know me, Stoksie. What do I care for twenty thousand? It's the principle of the thing.

Doc. That's what I say. *(Comes down to where Chub and Stokes are.)*

Chub. But Doc, are we not your best friends? Doesn't our friendship make Damon and Pythias look like a couple of pikers?

Doc. Yes, but Damon only had one Pythias. It makes a difference when you have a couple of Pythiases hanging on your neck.

Chub. Don't I share what I have with you—my ideas and everything? *(KNOCK on door. Doc pushes Chub in chair and hastily sticks thermometer in Chub's mouth and bends over him professionally, much to Chub's surprise. Mrs. Merrivale enters, leaning on Clem. She carries parrot perched on wrist or in a small cage.)*

Doc. Be a patient, Chub! Be a patient! Come right in, Mrs. Merrivale. *(Doc advances to meet her and assists her to chair L. of desk.)*

*(Mrs. Merrivale is a woman who imagines she is a chronic invalid and enjoys her misery immensely. Her greatest delight is to talk of her illnesses. She tries so hard to be a lady, and the bluntness of her daughter, Clementine, annoys and embarrasses her greatly. She walks with the aid of a cane, and makes a great fuss of it.)*

Mrs. Merrivale. Oh, Doctor, I had no idea you were engaged. You mustn't let me interrupt. Why didn't Mama's little girl tell me?

CLEM. They've been here half an hour. How did I know they was goin' to stay all day? *(MRS. MERRIVALE attempts to quiet her.)* I thought Doc was a fast worker. He always is on you.

MRS. MERRIVALE. Clementine! You must not be so tactless!

DOC. That's quite all right, Mrs. Merrivale—these gentlemen won't mind waiting, I'm sure. Just join the other patient in the waiting room. *(CHUB and STOKES sit on either side of small table at L. and pretend to read old magazines there. To her)* Unless you wish to see me in private?

MRS. MERRIVALE. Oh, no—no——

DOC. I'm very much interested in your case, Mrs. Merrivale. More interested than you know. *(MRS. MERRIVALE sits in chair L. of desk. CHUB and STOKES exchange glances and CLEM. looks suspicious. She stands by her mother's chair.)*

MRS. MERRIVALE. That is so kind of you, Doctor, but really, while I'm not a bit well—in fact, I'm all unstrung—it isn't myself I'm worried about to-day. It's another member of the family.

CLEM. But Maw, I ain't sick.

MRS. MERRIVALE. No, dear, of course you're not. You're always well. *(To Doc)* I don't know what I'd do without my little one. She's getting to be quite a help.

CLEM. *(Who never lets anybody get away with anything)* Help? Help! If you ask me, I'm the whole works!

MRS. MERRIVALE. *(Embarrassed)* She will have her little joke.

CLEM. Yes, that's one thing about me. *(Sarcastically)* I will have my little joke. You notice I'm laughing myself to death, don't you? *(CHUB and STOKES are sitting by the table and pretend to be reading literature there, but exchange side glances at each other.)*

Doc. Oh, Clementine!

Mrs. Merrivale. *(Ignoring what* Clem *says with difficulty)* No, Doctor, it isn't myself this time. It's the bird, Pollyanna.

Clem. The parrot? Oh, my Gawd!

Mrs. Merrivale. Clementine, say what you may, Pollyanna is not a well bird.

Clem. Do you mean to say that you brought that Irish Eagle to Doc?

Mrs. Merrivale. Why, certainly. Pollyanna is sick, I tell you. Clementine is absolutely lacking in sympathy for the sick and suffering.

Clem. Well, she ain't lacking in work, I notice.

Mrs. Merrivale. *Isn't,* dear—not *ain't.*

Clem. Well, maybe you isn't, but I ain't. I'm the only one in this house who ain't got time to be sick. Even the parrot can pull it—but not me!

Mrs. Merrivale. Petty!

Clem. Honest to Gawd, Doc, when I come up and asked you if you could see Maw, I didn't know it was about that bird. That's an awful insult, Doc, even to you. *(Exits* L.)

Mrs. Merrivale. Doctor, you don't mind my bringing my precious Pollyanna to you?

Doc. N-no—I'm glad you did. (Chub *and* Stokes *laugh.* Mrs. Merrivale *is indignant and stares at them.)*

Mrs. Merrivale. I love this bird, Doctor—I mean, Doctor, I love this bird, and I know she is ill. Only one who suffers as I do could feel it. (Mrs. Merrivale *groans and presses hand to side. It is obvious she is not in real pain. It is done for effect and is force of habit.)*

Doc. What is it? What's the matter?

Mrs. Merrivale. Oh! My poor liver. Doctor, sometimes I think my trouble is too deep for any medicine. If it weren't for my personal regard for you, I should certainly try an oyster bath. *(Groans and presses hand to other side)* Why don't you operate and be done with it?

Doc. I hope it isn't as serious as that.

Mrs. Merrivale. *(Abused)* It's very funny. I'm the only woman of my age in the entire block who hasn't had an operation.

Doc. Well, about the bird—— What symptoms have you observed? (Boys *laugh.* Doc *pretending to be very solicitous but in reality afraid of the parrot.)*

Mrs. Merrivale. Well, you know how talkative Pollyanna is? She hasn't spoken in two days. *(Said with an air of great calamity. If it is a real bird, Doc can get laughs by poking his finger at it and drawing it away quickly in fear.)* The little pet is so playful.

Doc. Indeed! Of course, Mrs. Merrivale, you realize I'm not a bird doctor.

Mrs. Merrivale. *(Apologetically)* Of course not! But I thought perhaps you could take it to a hospital—a bird hospital, and have it examined—I think it's adenoids.

Doc. Certainly I will.

Mrs. Merrivale. You're so kind, Doctor. You know, neither Pollyanna or I weren't able to eat a bite of breakfast, so I brought one of her favorite crackers. I thought it might keep her from being homesick at the hospital. *(Gets up, drops cane and gives a shrill little shriek.)*

Doc. What is it now?

Mrs. Merrivale. My poor heart, Doctor! My poor heart! (Chub *and* Stokes *jump to assist her.)* Thank you. I can't walk without my cane. *(Looks* Chub *full in the face)* It was so good of you to squeeze me in between these gentlemen. Dear me, young man; you do look ill.

Chub. *(Surprised)* Who—me?

Mrs. Merrivale. *(To Doc)* What is the matter with him?

Doc. *(Quickly)* Lungs.

Mrs. Merrivale. His lungs? It may be that *my* lungs are affected and not my liver at all—what do you think?

Doc. I think—it may be both.

Mrs. Merrivale. *(Secretly pleased)* I've suspected it all along. Oh, well, there's no use complaining. One must bear it and smile. You will be good to Pollyanna, won't you, Doctor? *(She has left* Pollyanna *on the desk and starts to go.)*

Doc. Need you ask?

Mrs. Merrivale. *(To Chub)* Take care of yourself, young man! Rely on Doctor Hampton. He knows more new diseases than any doctor I ever had in the house. Good morning. *(She exits L.* Chub *and* Stokes *burst out laughing.)*

Chub. That's a new one—a bird doctor!

Doc. Dry up!

Stokes. And for treating her you get your room rent free? I wonder if she needs any legal advice?

Chub. So pretty Pollyanna is sick, is she? And they brought her to Doc. Poor Polly! Poor Polly!

Doc. *(Angry)* Cut it out!

Stokes. Now you've got her, what are you going to do with her, Doc? *(They gather about the bird, each a little timid, to handle it.* Doc *is* R. Chub *by desk.* Stokes L. *of desk.)*

Doc. Blamed if I know! *(A light dawns on him)* Say, Chub—— *(Puts hand on* Chub's *shoulder)* I was just thinking—it would be very unusual to pawn a parrot, wouldn't it? *(*All *look at each other for a moment in silence.)*

Chub. By George, that's right!

Stokes. Are parrots worth anything?

Doc. To hear them talk you'd think so.

STOKES. I wonder if we could get anything on a parrot?

CHUB. We ought to get enough for breakfast.

DOC. Suppose you try, Chub?

CHUB. I try? Why pick on me?

STOKES. Because, Chubby, it was your idea to do something unusual—here's your chance.

CHUB. All right, I'm game. *(Grabs his hat)* What's the idea?

STOKES. Go to Cohen—round the corner—he's our friend.

DOC. And if the landlady sees you, say you're taking it to a hospital.

CHUB. *(Taking the parrot)* All right—kiss Polly good-bye, boys—you may never see her again.

DOC. Here, Chub. Don't forget Polly's breakfast. *(Gives* CHUB *the cracker* MRS. MERRIVALE *brought in, which* CHUB *starts to eat as he goes)* Hey! That's Polly's cracker.

CHUB. Polly lost a cracker. *(As he exits L.)*

STOKES. Doc, do you think Cohen will come across?

DOC. Cohen ought to do something. We're such good customers of his. Here's the proof. *(Opens desk drawer and pulls out neat bundle of pawn tickets)* This—— *(Runs his finger over stock of tickets. They gather at desk and examine pawn tickets.)* Here's my stickpin. *(As he takes one pawn ticket after another)* My silk hat—my cane—— Here's my winter overcoat—some coat, too—— Gee, I looked great in that coat,—and my dress suit. Here's my fraternity pin. Holy smoke, I've been supporting you fellows——. Everything here seems to be mine.

STOKES. Don't worry, just go down the list and you'll see my little contribution. See, here's my frat pin—my watch—silk hat—dress suit.

DOC. The only person who hasn't much here is

Chub. Do you suppose that son of a gun is holding
out on us? He might have another suit of clothes
some place.

Stokes. Chub never did have *much* except his
ideas.

Doc. *(Sadly)* And we couldn't get a nickel on
those.

Stokes. *(Lights a cigarette, then quite a long
pause. Turns quickly to Doc)* Perhaps Cohen
won't. Say, Doc, I wonder if by any chance Pollyanna has that parrot disease.

Doc. What disease?

Stokes. You're a *fine* doctor. There's quite a
scare about it. Don't you read the papers?

Doc. *(Knowingly)* Oh, *that*—psilosis. No fear,
Stoksie. Pollyanna still has her feathers. Now, don't
even hold the thought. Chub had the right idea.
The thing is to *think* success.

Stokes. Well, I'm thinking hard enough. Cohen,
I want my breakfast—Cohen, I want my breakfast.

Doc. Cohen, have a heart! Cohen, have a heart.
*(There is another pause. CHUB enters L. hurriedly,
waving pawn ticket in the air.)*

Chub. Three dollars and ninety cents!

Stokes. Gee! That's a fortune.

Chub. Some financier, eh?

Doc. Well, come on—divvy up.

Chub. Well, here it is, one dollar and thirty cents
apiece. *(Has the even amount for each.)*

Stokes. Gee, we're plutocrats—come on let's go
out and squander. And a nice new crisp dollar bill
at that.

Chub. *(After a pause)* I'm going to have a
group of ham and eggs.

Doc. I'm going to wait and see what's on the
menu. *(They start to go. KNOCK.)* Come in.

Clem. *(Enters)* Doctor, I brought a lady to see
you.

Doc. A lady! Bring her right in. It never rains but it pours—dollar thirty cents and a patient! *(Crosses to R. of desk.)*

CLEM. *(Speaks off L.)* Just wait a minute, Miss, and I'll explain. *(To desk)* Listen! They're playing some game outside for the Red Cross. Tag—I think it is. *(The* BOYS *look at each other, realising something is coming off.)* I seen this lady—swell looking, too—I seen her standin' in front of the house, pinnin' flags on men's coats, and every guy she tags—coughs up——

CHUB. What kind of language do you call that, Clementine—"coughs up"?

CLEM. Medical language—I just wanted Doc to understand—cough up—get me, Doc?

Doc. Perfectly.

CLEM. It's the *grandest* cause and I thought you gentlemen would feel hurt if you weren't able to help.

STOKES. That's very sweet of you, Clem—very thoughtful.

CLEM. Yes—so I askt her up—*(Goes to door L.)* Come in, Miss. *(Enter* MARY *with flags and purse)* Gentlemen, let me introduce Miss——

MARY. Don't bother with the name—Tag Day is enough. I suppose it's very unusual to have anyone come into your office this way?

Doc. It certainly is. *(*CLEM *exits as the* BOYS *crowd about* MARY. *She is embarrassed; doesn't know whether to walk out or not. The more fuss they make over* MARY *the funnier it is when she gets their money.)*

MARY. Which is the Doctor?

Doc. At your service. *(Edging in front of* CHUB *and* STOKES.*)*

MARY. I must apologize for coming in like this.

STOKES. *(Pushing* CHUB *aside)* The pleasure is all ours.

MARY. Thank you. Is this gentleman a doctor too?

STOKES. No—I'm a lawyer.

MARY. *(Pointing at them as in the old rhyme)* Oh, how romantic—"doctor—lawyer—merchant, chief." *(To* CHUB*)* Is this gentleman a merchant or chief?

CHUB. *(In his anxiety to be seen by* MARY; *steps upon couch)* Why—er——

DOC. Either one—hot air merchant.

STOKES. Or Chief Clown!

MARY. That's very unkind.

CHUB. *(Stepping down)* As a matter of fact, I'm the financial man of the group.

MARY. *(Reaches in her bag for flag)* Oh, how lovely! Then I'll tag you first. (Doc *and* STOKES *back away, laughing, as* MARY *takes flag and pins it on* CHUB.)

CHUB. *(Looking foolishly from one to the other)* Pretty little flag, isn't it? *(*STOKES *and* Doc *pretend to take great interest in flag.)*

STOKES. Why, that's a beautiful flag, Chub.

DOC. I should say it is—that's something to be proud of, Chub. You certainly are a lucky fellow!

MARY. But all my flags are equally as pretty—I wouldn't think of slighting the doctor—*(Pins flag on* Doc, *much to his discomfort)*—or the lawyer—*(Pins flag on* STOKES*)*—there you are—no favoritism—see?

DOC. Yes—I see.

MARY. And now for my fee—first the doctor—he probably knows more about fees than anyone else.

DOC. *(Pulls out dollar bill and hands it to* MARY*)* How much?

MARY. Anything you like. *(Takes dollar bill)* That will do nicely. *(Turns quickly to* STOKES *as*

Doc *stands with hands out as if waiting for change)*
Now the lawyer.

STOKES. *(Giving dollar bill which* MARY *puts in bag)* Any change?

MARY. Change! Why, shame on you; and now for the best of all—the financier. (CHUB *has pulled out dollar bill with change at same time as* Doc *and* STOKES. *He tries to put back dollar but* MARY *sees change and dollar bill and deftly, without being bold, takes it all)* Lovely! I knew the financier would be best. *(The* BOYS *try to laugh.)* There, you are all decorated up.

Doc. And cleaned out!

MARY. I knew when I first came in I'd be successful.

CHUB. I had a hunch, too.

MARY. Professional men are always generous.

Doc. Well, you're no amateur yourself—you know.

MARY. I'd better go.

Doc. Don't go. You be a little generous, too.

MARY. You'll never regret this—it's really a wonderful charity.

Doc. It *must* be if you have anything to do with it.

MARY. This will mean food to many starving victims.

STOKES. Food? You'll give them food with that?

Doc. I'm glad someone gets food with that.

CHUB. I'm glad Polly had a cracker.

MARY. I hope I haven't taken too much of your time.

Doc. You haven't taken too much—time. It isn't the time.

CHUB. Does everyone give a dollar?

MARY. No, indeed.

STOKES. Oh, I see, we just had to——

MARY. Most men give much more, but it isn't the

amount that counts—it's the spirit in which it's given.

DOC. *(Very lamely)* Oh, yes—I see—the spirit.

CHUB. Well, we might as well be cheerful.

MARY. You remember the story of the widow's mite.

DOC. We're not widows—this is the story of the bachelor's roll.

MARY. Are you all bachelors?

STOKES. I am!

CHUB. *(Jumps to her R. Doc pulls CHUB violently aside and steps close to MARY)* I am!

DOC. I am—extremely! Are you, too?

MARY. Of course not——

DOC. But I mean——

MARY. Now I must go. *(Backs away L.)*

DOC. Not before you tell me.

MARY. Why, what possible difference could it make?

DOC. *(Following her)* What difference—a lot of difference—please tell me your name.

MARY. Why?

DOC. Well, you may need a doctor some time.

STOKES. *(They line up facing MARY. Doc first, STOKES second, CHUB behind STOKES)* Or a lawyer.

CHUB. Or a financier.

MARY. *(Amused)* If I do I shall call on my three cavaliers.

DOC. But the name?

MARY. Do you really want my name?

*(Door L. opens and MRS. BURNS, superbly dressed, enters, following CLEM.)*

CLEM. Is this her, Ma'm?

MRS. BURNS. *(Standing L. a little down stage)* My dear, I've been looking everywhere for you. If it hadn't been for this young woman I should have gone off and left you——

MARY. I was just coming. Let me introduce the doctor, the lawyer and the merchant chief. *(They bow to* MRS. BURNS. *She bows in return.)*

MRS. BURNS. You know, my dear, this isn't at all ethical to come into a doctor's office and disturb him this way—even if it is for Charity.

DOC. Charity begins at home and anyway it's a pleasure, I assure you.

CHUB *and* STOKES. *(Forced)* Yes, indeed!

MARY. I was just thinking how wonderful it would be if all gentlemen were as easy to get money from as you are. *(Gives money to* MRS. BURNS. *A dollar bill flutters to the floor.* CHUB *and* STOKES *move but* MRS. BURNS *holds out her hand for* DOC *to give it to her.)*

MRS. BURNS. How splendid! Then I mustn't scold you so much after all. Success is it's own defence. *(Puts money in her bag.)*

MARY. I wanted to make a record.

DOC. Well, you have.

MRS. BURNS. It's very sweet of you to take it so good-naturedly, but she shouldn't do it. Good day. Come, dear.

DOC. But Miss—mayn't I see you to the door?

MRS. BURNS. Don't bother—good day. *(*MARY *extends her hand. The* BOYS *rush forward to take it.* DOC *gets it first and kisses it.)*

DOC. *(Opening door)* I must see you out. *(*MARY, MRS. BURNS *and* DOC *exit* L.*)*

STOKES. *(Pointing to his flag)* A dollar for that.

CHUB. *(Touching his)* A dollar-thirty cents for this.

STOKES. The widow's mite.

CHUB. Well, it was a good cause.

STOKES. I never realized before how much the

poor have suffered. Say, whose idea was it to give a dollar?

Doc. *(Entering enthusiastically)* Gee, wasn't she a peach! *(He goes to* L. *window. They follow him.)* There she is getting in a car—a Rolls, too—some rich girl—I suppose—just my luck!

Stokes. Just his luck! Can you beat that? Just your luck! She wouldn't even give you her name.

Doc. *(Swaggers to* C.*)* Name? Name? What's in a name? Did you see the way she looked at me when she left?

Stokes. *(Crossing to* Doc*)* Doc—I didn't know that you were conceited before. I was the one she looked at.

Doc. You—that's funny—she didn't know you were alive. I'll leave it to Chub—— Who did she look at as she left this room?

Chub. *(Still at window)* At me, of course.

Doc. *(Goes to desk; sits on edge)* Well, I'll prove it. I'll show you fellows. No hands but hers shall ever touch this flag! I'll find her if I have to scour New York. *(They laugh.)* Don't laugh. I'll find her and then—who knows—every young doctor should have a wife, anyway.

Stokes. That's funny—a wife! Ha—ha! How could you support a wife? You can't even support me.

Doc. Why talk about money in connection with a girl like that?

Chub. *(Now on couch)* After the way she cleaned us out, why talk about anything else?

Doc. Why, I'd beg, borrow or steal for a girl like that.

Stokes. *(Now* L. *of desk)* Doc—I never suspected this of you. I always thought you were pretty well balanced, but gee, if the mere sight of a pretty face affects you this way——

ACT I

See page 38

Doc. It isn't that. Here I am, all broke and everything, and she had to come along.

Stokes. And *she* broke you—don't forget that!

Doc. *(Picking up uncle's letter and shaking his fist at it)* I suppose if I had a large practice and all the money I wanted, old G. P. would send me a house and lot for a wedding present. (Chub *gets idea.*)

Stokes. Them that *has,* gets.

Doc. Yes, and I suppose all the rest of the family would send on silver and cut-glass and all sorts of valuable stuff, but now, when I need it to keep from starving, not a nickel can I get from them.

Chub. *(Rises, as though he had an inspiration)* Wait a minute—— I have an idea. Do you think they'd really send on presents if you were going to be married?

Doc. Why, of course they would. Everybody always does, don't they?

Chub. *(Walking toward Doc and Stokes)* That's right. It's inborn in the human race. People just don't dare not to send a wedding present—it's an acknowledgment of poverty or meanness. Now, if we sent wedding invitations to your rich relatives in Fargo, they would think you were going to be married, and would send on presents just the same as if you really *were* to be married. *(Seeing they are beginning to grasp the idea and warming up to the subject. The possibility of the thing dawns on* Doc *and* Stokes *and they rush to* Chub *with one accord.)* And they are sure to send something valuable. It's always a check or jewelry—or silver—or cut-glass. And when the presents come, we can pawn them.

Doc. Oh, I see—*I* get them, but *we* pawn them.

Chub. Well, isn't it *my* idea?

Doc. I don't care—I'll split. I'll do anything to

get a bankroll and find that girl. It's a great scheme, Chub. You're all right.

STOKES. Wait a minute.

Doc. Here's old legal gloom. What's the obstacle?

STOKES. *(Very grandly)* I'm a lawyer and my training naturally teaches me to see all sides of a question.

Doc. Well, quit bragging—and let's have the obstacle.

STOKES. Who's the bride? It's a criminal offense to use anybody's name.

CHUB. Take a fictitious name—something that no one could object to.

Doc. Sure! Some common name. Brown—Greene—or Jones or Smith.

CHUB. I'll duck out in the hall and get the telephone book. I won't be a minute. *(Exits L.)*

STOKES. Remember now—as your attorney. I advise against this.

Doc. Come out of it! You won't advise against accepting some of the money when we pawn the presents, though, will you?

STOKES. *(His need of money overcoming his judgment)* Well, of course I'll help you all I can—but remember, I advised against it.

Doc. What are you talking about? It's a great scheme.

CHUB. *(Enters L. Going to desk, R. chair. Doc stands behind desk upstage. STOKES L. of desk)* Here we are! Brown first. One—two—three—four —five—six—seven—almost eight columns of Browns.

STOKES. How many Greenes?

Doc. *(Sarcastically)* How many Greenes? You'd think he was selling vegetables.

CHUB. Greene—Greene—— *(Turning pages of book to "Greene")* One—two—three—only three

columns of Greene. The Browns outcolor the
Greenes.

Doc. How about Jones?

Chub. *(Turning to Jones)* Jones—Jones—ah,
one—two—three—four—five—five Jones.

Stokes. Better than the Greenes—but the
Browns still have it.

Chub. Yes, looks like you'll marry a Brown.

Doc. Try Smiths now—let's give all the girls a
chance.

Chub. *(Turning to Smiths)* Here we are——
One, two, three, four, five, six, seven, eight, nine,
ten, eleven, twelve—twelve columns of Smiths.
There's a name for you.

Doc. *(Crossing dramatically to c.)* Pass the
Browns—I shall marry me a Smith. *(Doubtfully)*
It isn't very romantic, though, Smith, huh? What
do you think?

Chub. Well, Greene is romantic—it suggests
spring and in the spring a young man's fancy—you
know——

Stokes. Or Brown—that's a nice color—unless
it's too dark.

Doc. No—I'll have no dark-brown bride.

Stokes. Smith is safer. As your attorney, I
recommend Smith.

Doc. All right! Smith it is.

Stokes. Now let's frame the invitation. Who
knows how they read?

Chub. I do. I read one once. Gather round.
*(They all huddle over desk. Writes)* Mr. and Mrs.
Smith——

Stokes. There should be an initial there.

Doc. All right—let them have an initial. I think
a "J" would look pretty—don't you?

Chub. "J." would stand for Joseph.

Chub. Or just plain J-A-Y!

Stokes. Yes—"J." is safe.

Doc. And very appropriate.

Chub. All right. There are a lot of Jays in the world. *(Writes)* Mr. and Mrs. J. Smith request the pleasure of your company at the marriage of their daughter—— What's the bride's name, anyway?

Stokes. Make it something safe.

Doc. Like Cleopatra? I don't think she would object.

Chub. That sounds pretty too. Cleopatra Smith will marry Anthony Hampton.

Doc. Let's think of the commonest name in the world.

Stokes. *(Going down the alphabet)* Alice, Beatrice, Carrie, Dora, Emma, Fannie, Gertrude, Helen.

Chub. Let's give her two names, like Alice Beatrice, or Carrie Dora, or Emma Fannie.

Doc. You'll do nothing of the sort. I'm marrying the girl. I'll call her what I please. It will be—— Let's think—— It will be—Mary Jane—that's it.

Stokes. That certainly sounds safe—Mary Jane Smith.

Chub. Safe enough, right! *(With irony.)*

Stokes. Now, let's have it again.

Chub. *(Reads)* Mr. and Mrs. J. Smith request—

Stokes. There should be an address there.

Doc. *(Exasperated)* You can cause more trouble!

Stokes. You want this thing to be right, don't you? They must live somewhere.

Doc. Smiths live everywhere.

Chub. *(With the air of one settling an argument)* All right. We'll take you to Jersey. How about Elizabeth, New Jersey? *(Reads)* Mr. and Mrs. J. Smith of—Main Street, Elizabeth, New Jersey.

Stokes. Has Elizabeth a Main Street?

Doc. Every town has a Main Street.

Chub. Main Street, Elizabeth, New Jersey, re-

quest the pleasure of your company—*(Looks at
Doc)* —at the marriage of their daughter, Mary
Jane Smith, to George Hampton, M.D.

STOKES. Wait a minute! These invitations should
be engraved, you know.

CHUB. I know a place where they print them so
it looks just like engraving—you can hardly tell.

DOC. I've got to hand it to you, Chub. It's a
great scheme, all right. You're a wonder.

CHUB. It's nice to be appreciated, Doc.

STOKES. Too bad we haven't a drink to toast the
bride.

DOC. Let's see. I have some nice prussic acid—
some glycothermaline.

CHUB. Well, boys—things are picking up.

DOC. Let's go out and eat. *(They start to go.)*

CHUB. Eat! Now there is a *word.* Wait a minute. How much money you got, Doc? (CHUB *is* c.
STOKES R. DOC L.)               *(WARN Curtain.)*

DOC. Thirty cents. *(Showing it.)*

CHUB. How much you got, Stoksie?

STOKES. I got thirty cents, too. *(Showing it.)*

CHUB. *(Taking a dime from each)* There, now!
That's settled.

DOC. You ought to get along all right doing business that way. We're out a dime apiece.

CHUB. What do you care for a dime?

STOKES. Yes! What do we care so long as you
get it?

CHUB. Come on! You got money in the pocket,
ideas in the head and song in the heart.

STOKES. Yes! Song o' six-pence!

DOC. No, the wedding march. Here comes the
bride! *(They join hands and start singing "Here
Comes the Bride." Just as they get to door with a
loud "Here Comes the Bride,"* CLEM *opens door
suddenly; has dustpan, duster, and cloth for veil.)*

CLEM. Can I clean your room out now?

Doc. Sure! We're cleaned out—so why not clean out the room. (Doc *grabs* CLEM'S *arm and* BOYS *follow in rear as bridesmaids holding her dress, singing "Here Comes the Bride." As they make circle of stage and exit,* CHUB *takes* CLEM'S *dustpan and holds it like bridal bouquet.* STOKES *does the same with the feather-duster.)*

## CURTAIN

# ACT TWO

SCENE: *Same as Act I.*
    *Stage is empty as Curtain rises. There is a KNOCK on door. This is repeated several times. Enter CLEM with telegram.*
    *Couch should be a little more C. and the DOCTOR'S bag is still in place on desk or floor R.*

CLEM. *(Sticking head around door)* Doctor Hampton! Doctor Hampton! Here's a telegram for you. *(No answer. She comes in room, leaving the door open)* Doctor Hampton! *(Walks to desk and puts telegram against blotter. She notices desk is dusty and wipes it off with her apron. While she is doing this she accidentally pushes wedding invitation envelope on floor. She picks it up and glances at it, feels it and then looks carelessly in envelope, as she sees it is not sealed. Glances at door and walks nonchalantly over and closes it. Stands with back to door and reads wedding invitation. Her surprise makes her walk a step or two from door, and while she is reading CHUB comes rushing in L., knocking her over. She hastily puts invitation in apron pocket.)*

CHUB. *(Down C.)* I beg your pardon—— Oh, it's you, Clementine.

CLEM. *(Bending over chair, dusting)* Yes, it's me, and who give you the right to call me Clementine?

CHUB. Why—er——

CLEM. You wouldn't think of calling my mother *Madeline,* would you?

39

CHUB. No, I don't think I would.

CLEM. Well, just because I work for a livin' don't give nobody no right to be familiar.

CHUB. I'm sorry, I'm sure. It's only because I've heard Doctor Hampton call you Clementine.

CLEM. *(As she rises from her knees)* Yes—but, if a certain thing I suspect is true, he better quit callin' me Clementine any more.

CHUB. What do you mean?

CLEM. I ain't sayin' a word, but I'm goin' to keep a sharp eye on this room from now on. *(She starts to go. Crosses to closet door and looks in to see if there are any women's clothes hanging there.)* Mr.—— Oh! Pardon me—what's your name?

CHUB. *(Below desk)* My name is Perkins— Harry Perkins.

CLEM. Well, Mr. Perkins, will you see Doctor Hampton gets that telegram on the desk?

CHUB. Yes, I will, Clementine.

CLEM. *(Angry because he uses her first name)* Thank you, *Harry.*

CHUB. *(Apologetically)* Miss Merrivale.

CLEM. *Mr.* Perkins. *(She exits* L. CHUB *follows, bowing exaggeratedly as* DOC *enters.)*

CHUB. Excuse me. *(Bows)* I beg your pardon. *(Bows.)*

DOC. *(Entering from* L.*)* What's the idea? *(He has some papers in his hands.)*

CHUB. I was bowing to Miss Merrivale.

DOC. Forget Clementine. I'm worried about the landlady. *(At* R. *of desk.* CHUB *at* L.*)* She insists on hearing every day how that fool parrot Pollyanna is getting along. *(Takes out envelope with ticket in it and lays it on top of desk)* She's so engrossed with the parrot's condition she has almost forgotten to be sick herself.

CHUB. That will never do.

DOC. *(Crosses to* C. *below desk where* CHUB *is)*

I should say not. I—I gave her a book on symptoms the other day. There are some diseases in it she'll be crazy about, I know. Of course you realize it would be unprofessional for me to suggest a disease—but I can't help it if she discovers them herself—and—I must have some place to sleep.

CHUB. Sure. At least until the presents come.

Doc. Presents! I don't want to be a killjoy, but it's nine days since we sent out those wedding invitations. It's three days there and three days back. That is allowing them three days for shopping.

CHUB. But perhaps they're having the silver engraved. *(Takes out pipe and empty pouch; prepares to smoke.)*

Doc. The silver? You seem certain of the silver.

CHUB. There is always silver.             -

Doc. Is there? Want a match?

CHUB. *(Starts to fill pipe and discovers there is no tobacco. Tries to put it away without Doc seeing)* No, I've changed my mind.

Doc. *(Examines pouch. Seeing CHUB has no tobacco)* Gee, Chub, is it as bad as that?

CHUB. I don't want to smoke, anyway. It's a rotten habit when you come right down to it.

Doc. Have a cigarette?

CHUB. Well, if you can spare it. (Doc *opens box and hands it to CHUB. CHUB looks inside)* There's only one here.

Doc. The last of the Egyptians! Go ahead, Chub. Take it. I'm off the Oriental stuff, anyway.

CHUB. No—I don't want it. I'm superstitious.

Doc. I'll split with you. (Doc *divides cigarette with CHUB; lights CHUB's and he takes long puffs.)* Funny how good the last one tastes.

CHUB. You're lucky to have the last one.

Doc. Chub, do something for me, will you?

CHUB. After such generosity—*(Indicating butt of cigarette)* —how can I refuse?

Doc. I brought some charts from the hospital.
I'll pretend they are reports on Pollyanna's condition and read them to the landlady. Fill one out
for me. (Chub *takes pen and writes. Doc crosses
to* R. *of desk and sits)* Put down—— Let's see,
now. I must make her better or worse.

Chub. Make her worse.

Doc. All right. Put down twenty opposite respiration.

Chub. Have parrots got a respiration?

Doc. They seem to have everything else. Put
down one hundred and three temperature and——

(Mrs. Merrivale *enters* L. *without knocking. She
is leaning heavily on cane, evidently very much
excited.)*

Mrs. Merrivale. Excuse me for not knocking,
Doctor. I'm all upset.

Doc. What's the trouble?

Mrs. Merrivale. I didn't realize how I've suffered all these years until I read this book, but now
no matter how well I seem I'll never feel safe
again. I have every disease but two.

Doc. Which two are those? (*Takes book from
her.)*

Mrs. Merrivale. Hydrophobia and shingles. I
realize now there's no hope for me. (Doc *and*
Chub *exchange glances and* Chub *makes motion to
tear up Pollyanna's report, but* Doc *grabs it from
his hand.)* But then, there's no use complaining. I
must bear it and smile. (Doc *gives sigh of relief.)*

Chub. That's the way to talk—be cheerful—
that's my motto.

Doc. Now we're all happy and—— *(Forced
laugh.)*

Mrs. Merrivale. Doctor, how is Pollyanna?

Doc. (*His happiness disappearing abruptly)* Oh!

Let me see. I have her report right on my desk
here.

MRS. MERRIVALE. *(Drops hot-water bottle. Before he can proceed)* Tell me the worst——

DOC. I always do—I assure you.

MRS. MERRIVALE. You're so kind. (DOC *crosses
up back of desk. As he picks up chart from desk*
CLEM *enters* L. CHUB *and* DOC *can tell from her
manner something unusual is about to come off.)*

CLEM. Oh, Maw! I've been lookin' for you.
There is something about somebody you ought to
know. (DOC *and* CHUB *stare straight ahead, afraid
to glance at each other.)*

MRS. MERRIVALE. Whatever it is, you must wait
until I hear of Pollyanna's condition. *(Sits* L. *of
desk.)*

CLEM. I'll wait. *(Looks severely at* DOC; *sits on
couch.)*

DOC. *(Uncomfortable under her gaze)* Respiration, nineteen.

CHUB. No, I put down twenty.

DOC. That's right—respiration, twenty.

CLEM. I didn't know parrots perspired.

MRS. MERRIVALE. *(Annoyed and humiliated)*
Respiration—not perspiration.

CLEM. *(In doubt)* I thought it was perspiration.
*(With sudden conviction)* It is perspiration!

MRS. MERRIVALE. Oh, do be quiet. You don't
even know what the doctor means.

CLEM. I certainly do know what he means. It's
when you work hard like I do—and the water comes
out of your little pores——

CHUB. That's what I call clever, Clementine.

CLEM. Yes, *Harry!* But I never heard of a parrot perspiring.

CHUB. Well, you can hardly blame it—with all
those feathers on.

CLEM. I guess you're right.

Mrs. Merrivale. You do humiliate me so——
Go on, Doctor.

Doc. Temperature, one hundred and three.

Mrs. Merrivale. One hundred and three? That's
very high, isn't it? Why, the hottest day we had
last summer—it was only ninety-eight!

Clem. Temperature! A parrot's temperature?
How do you take temperature?

Doc. I take one of these ther——

Clem. *(Looking at thermometer closely)* That's
made of glass, isn't it?

Doc. *(Timidly)* Yes, indeed. I just place this
end in the mouth——

Clem. *(Crooking her finger in shape of parrot's
beak)* Let me get this right, Doc. You place *that*
in a parrot's mouth? Why, that bird thinks a Bra-
zillian nut is a piece of marshmallow and you tell
me you put that in its mouth? If you did, all I can
say is, Pollyanna has changed. .

Mrs. Merrivale. *(Utterly humiliated and exasperated)* Doctor, I apologize. Do you wonder why
my nerves are unstrung?

Clem. Do I unstring your nerves, Maw?

Mrs. Merrivale. *(Almost in tears)* You certainly do!

Clem. Well, your nerves will need restringin'
when you hear what's comin'. So prepare yourself
for a shock. As far as we know, there ain't been no
woman hangin' around here.

Mrs. Merrivale. *"Isn't,"* not "ain't"! Don't be
*ungrammarical!*

Clem. Grammar ain't got nothin' to do with a
case like this. This affair is respectable or it ain't
—that's all.

Mrs. Merrivale. Clementine! You *are* aggra-
vating.

Clem. *But* careful! Mind you, Doctor Hampton
—and I'm sayin' this in front of a witness——

*(To* CHUB*)* You're a witness. I ain't accusin' you
of nothin'—remember that.

MRS. MERRIVALE. Don't get me all worked up,
Clementine.

CLEM. Huh! To mention you and work is funny.

MRS. MERRIVALE. There she goes again. *(To*
DOC*)* I can't even speak to her lately without her
snapping at me in that vulgar, offensive way. It's
really dreadful, and me an invalid. Oh, to think I
should raise a child to talk like that to me!

CLEM. *(Rising)* Don't get heroic, Maw—yet.
Save your strength. Something tells me you are going to need it. Read this! *(Dramatically produces
wedding invitation.* DOC, *who has been trying to
pacify them during their quarrel, starts to look for
wedding invitation.* CHUB *also.)*

MRS. MERRIVALE. It's a wedding invitation!

DOC. *(To* CLEM*)* Where did you get that?
*(Then turns to* CHUB *and they whisper.)*

CLEM. I got it—that's enough.

MRS. MERRIVALE. *(Reading; as she comes to*
DOCTOR's *name she reads aloud)* "Mary Jane Smith
to George Hampton, M.D."

CLEM. Those invitations are dated a week ago.
I've looked all over this room and there is no
woman's clothes I can find. It's very unusual.

MRS. MERRIVALE. *(Suddenly rises)* If he is married, he'll leave—then—what's to become of me?

CLEM. You surprise me, Maw.

MRS. MERRIVALE. You don't care what happens
to me—my own child doesn't care what happens
to me.

DOC. *(Coming down to her, forming a line across
the stage—*MRS. MERRIVALE R., *then* DOC, CHUB
*and* CLEM*)* But I'm not married.

CLEM. You're not?

DOC. I give you my word of honor, I am not
married.

MRS. MERRIVALE. *(With arm outstretched to Doc)* Promise me—promise me, you won't give up this room and leave me.

DOC. Never!

MRS. MERRIVALE. Promise you won't leave me!

CLEM. For Gawd's sake, Maw, control yourself. Anybody would think there was something between you two.

MRS. MERRIVALE. *(Screams)* Oh, I'm going to faint!

CLEM. *(Terrified)* Don't faint, Maw. Don't faint. (MRS. MERRIVALE *knows from experience that* CLEM *is afraid of fainting and promptly does so.)*

DOC. Chub, get me those smelling-salts. *(Slaps her wrists.* CHUB *gets salts and holds them under* MRS. MERRIVALE'S *nose.)*

CLEM. *(To* DOC*)* You can have a hundred wives and keep the whole bunch hid—for all I care. Maw! (MRS. MERRIVALE *opens eyes dramatically.)*

DOC. *(Speaking so* MRS. MERRIVALE *will hear)* But—I will not get married.

MRS. MERRIVALE. *(Weakly)* But you mustn't—let me—spoil your life.

DOC. (CLEM *starts up* C.) My duty comes first.

MRS. MERRIVALE. Isn't he noble? *(Recovering very suddenly.)*

DOC. I will not get married! Give up this room —just when I need—I'm needed most? Never! Never! (MRS. MERRIVALE *cries.* CHUB *grasps* Doc's hand heroically. CLEM *is dumfounded.)*

CLEM. Who started this, anyway? Come on, Maw. (MRS. MERRIVALE *rises with aid of cane and takes* CLEM's *arm.)* I'll never open my face again as long as I live.

MRS. MERRIVALE. Here's your invitation, Doctor. *(Gives him invitation.)*

Doc. I was going to send that invitation to you, Mrs. Merrivale.

Mrs. Merrivale. Don't do it, Doctor! It isn't that I'm not grateful for you thinking of me—but I can't afford a present.

Chub. *(Unable to repress himself)* Ah ha!

Clem. What do you mean by "Ah ha"? It's no disgrace for me and Maw to be poor.

Doc. The wedding has been indefinitely postponed.

Mrs. Merrivale. *(Putting hand on Doc's shoulder)* Oh, Doctor!

Clem. *(To Chub)* I hope you're broad-minded.

Mrs. Merrivale. I almost forgot. Will you as a special favor bring Pollyanna home?

Doc. When?

Mrs. Merrivale. Today.

Doc. *(Exchanges looks with Chub)* But—but—it may be dangerous to remove her so soon.

Mrs. Merrivale. Dangerous? But if I wasn't with her in her last hours I'd never forgive myself. The poor little lonely bird. (Mrs. Merrivale *and* Clem *exit* L.)

Chub. *(Crossing to Doc. They stand up c.)* The presents are bound to come. Did you hear what she said about the invitation?

Doc. But did you hear what she said about the parrot?

Chub. What are you going to do?

Doc. *(Speaks in whisper)* You go around to Cohen and see how Pollyanna is. Maybe she really is dead.

*(Enter Stokes L. as Doc is giving Chub his hat. He hears the word "dead.")*

Stokes. Hello, boys!

Doc. Sst—— *(Finger to lips)* Not a word. *(To* Chub*)* Hurry.

Chub. All right. I'll see if she's dead.

Doc. And if she is, bring the body home. *(*Stokes *starts.* Chub *exits* l. *very mysteriously.)*

Stokes. What's the mystery?

Doc. Ssh—— *(Peeps around door cautiously)* I'm glad you came.

Stokes. Have you murdered somebody? *(They speak in whispers.)*

Doc. Ssh!

Stokes. Say, I'm going. *(Starts to door.)*

Doc. *(Holding him back)* No—I may need your help.

Stokes. What's it all about?

Doc. It's—no—I can't tell you.

Stokes. *(Indignantly)* What! Have you ever known me to betray the confidence of a client before?

Doc. I never knew you to have a client before.

Stokes. Of course, if you feel that way about it. *(His curiosity gets the better of him.)* Oh, come on. Give us a tell.

Doc. It's the landlady.

Stokes. Don't tell me she's dead.

Doc. She wants Pollyanna brought home today.

Stokes. I thought maybe she was dead and you'd lost your room.

Doc. That's decent of you, Stokes, to have my welfare at heart.

Stokes. Yes, I wanted you to put me up till Saturday. My landlady has seized my trunk and locked my room.

Doc. Till Saturday—— That reminds me I have been eating across the street this week and my board's due Saturday—so if the presents don't come——

ACT II

See page 56

STOKES. *(Crossing L.)* What do you suppose is causing the delay?

DOC. They're having the silver engraved.

CLEM. *(Enters L.)* There's an expressman with some packages for you.

*(Enter EXPRESSMAN with seven packages as CLEM motions him in.)*

EXPRESSMAN. Expecting anything?

DOC. Well, yes—from Fargo.

EXPRESSMAN. *(Packages being rather bulky are put on floor)* That's right. Sign here. (Doc *signs.*)

CLEM. Have you heard about the parrot?

DOC. *(Joyfully)* Pollyanna? Yes, indeed, and I'm glad to say she's greatly improved. *(Looking at presents)* In fact I think, from present indications, she'll be home this afternoon. (STOKES *grins.* EXPRESSMAN *glares at him.*)

CLEM. I'm glad of that. It's all Maw can talk about. (CLEM *looks at* EXPRESSMAN *waiting for tip)* No chance. *(She exits.* EXPRESSMAN *exits with look look of disgust because he didn't get a tip.* Doc *and* STOKES *rush to parcels with one accord.)*

DOC. What did I tell you? It worked! We'll be on Easy Street—when we pawn these——

STOKES. This must be from old G. P. It's so tight. Got some scissors?

DOC. *(Getting cutter from desk)* Here—take this. It's for cutting out tonsils—but it's all right.

STOKES. I'll bet it was like cutting out old G. P.'s tonsils to separate him from what's in here. Heavy, too!

DOC. Gee, I wish Chub was here! *(During this scene they cut open strings of packages quickly and begin to unwrap parcels as fast as possible.)*

STOKES. No—I'm wrong—this is not from G. P. It says on the box, "Mrs. Oliver Hampton."

Doc. My Aunt Jane—— Isn't that thoughtful of dear Aunt Jane? She's so sensible—and has such good taste. She's rich, too. I'll bet we live a week on what Aunt Jane sent.

Stokes. Well—lift the lid on Aunt Jane. *(Reads card)* "To dear Mary from Aunt Jane." *(Takes cover off box and takes out beautiful hand-made nightdress.)*

Doc. Good Lord!

Stokes. Oh, yes—we'll live a week on that. We might live a week in it.

Doc. *(Takes gown)* That's a foolish present— unless it's filled. Well—maybe we'll have better luck here. *(Reads card in another box)* "From Cousin Grace." *(Pulls out Japanese pajama suit, jacket and trousers, elaborately embroidered. They are dumfounded.)* They must think I married a Jap.

Stokes. *(Opening another box, pulling lingerie out. Doc grabs it from him with shocked expression and returns it to box)* That's an insult, that is. *(Meaning combination or a "Teddy" and pair of bloomers.)*

Doc. It's for Mary.

Stokes. Oh, that's different.

Doc. *What?* Why, everything here is for Mary.

Stokes. You certainly are popular with your own family.

Doc. I can't understand it—I'm dazed.

Stokes. *(Pulling out contents of another box)* Linen hand-made towels. Everything they sent is sort of boudoiry, isn't it? Where is the jewelry and the cut glass and the silver with the initials on?

Doc. *(Takes out punch-bowl or vase)* Here's something heavy—cut glass. *(He opens it and in his haste drops it and breaks it. There should be an iron under rug to be sure glass breaks.)*

Stokes. The only thing we could possibly pawn

and you have to break it! Wait a minute—here's one we overlooked.

Doc. Oh, that's too small.

Stokes. It says "valuables" on the outside.

Doc. (*Grabs it—reads card*) "To dear Mary, my new niece, these priceless jewels——" *(They both jump with joy and shake hands. He reads on)* "Their actual value is practically nothing, but they will be priceless to you because they have been in the family for many generations." *(They are dazed.)*

Stokes. (*Sarcastically*) Well, it certainly was a great scheme.

Doc. (*Throws pillow at his head*) Dry up. I wonder what's keeping Chub. (Chub *enters, breathless and full of news.*) Ah ha! Here's our little playmate.

Chub. (*All excited*) Cohen says we can't have the bird till we pay a bill of five dollars for board!

Stokes. Board?

Chub. He says never in his life has he seen such an appetite.

Doc. That's the last straw——

Chub. And he—— *(To* Doc*)* —says he has lost a lot of customers through the parrot's swearing and he is going to sue us. He says the blamed thing has eaten up all his interest.

Stokes. We have good news, too. The presents have come!

Chub. They have?

Stokes. They have!

Doc. (*Crossing* r. *of* Chub) They have!

Chub. I tell you it's very gratifying to conceive an idea and have it turn out this way. Some day you fellows will give me credit.

Doc. Yes, we're going to give it to you in just a minute, Chub—all the credit you deserve. Stokes, shall we show him the presents now?

STOKES. It wouldn't be fair not to show them.

CHUB. Come on—quit stalling.

DOC. Is there anybody you would like to have notified?

CHUB. *(Trying to back away. Doc seizes one arm and STOKES the other)* What are you doing, kidding me?

DOC. Oh, no, you don't! Look! Gaze! Drink it in. Those are the valuable presents you promised.

STOKES. This!

DOC. And that! *(Showing him present.)*

STOKES. And these. *(Showing him present.)*

DOC. And those! *(Showing him present.)*

STOKES. And them!

CHUB. Where's the silver?

DOC. They're having it engraved.

CHUB. My—my brain's in a whirl!

DOC. Your brain! Your brain is so big you could wear a demi-tasse for a high hat—and then you'd have to pad it. *(Crosses R., front of desk.)*

CHUB. But G. P.—your uncle—didn't—didn't he send anything?

DOC. Not even a wire of congratulation——

CHUB. *(Starts R.)* Oh, a wire——

DOC. Shut up! *(Pushes CHUB into chair L. of desk.)*

STOKES. *(Simultaneously)* Keep still! *(CHUB hands wire on desk to Doc after furtive glance at Doc and STOKES.)*

DOC. When did this come?

CHUB. *(Not sure he will be allowed to speak, as Doc is standing in a threatening attitude on one side and STOKES on the other)* Clementine brought it in w—when you were out this m—morning.

STOKES. You're certainly a great help to have around, Chub.

CHUB. Read it. Maybe it's from your uncle.

DOC. Yes, Bright Eyes, maybe it is. *(Reads tele-*

*gram)* "Arrive at three en route to Bermuda. Sailing on The Bermudian at five. Will stop on way to boat to meet your wife. Have wedding present with me. G. P. Hampton."

CHUB. At three. *(Looks at watch)* He's in town now.

Doc. What have I done to deserve this?

STOKES. It certainly was a great scheme. Where shall I *put* these *valuable* presents?

Doc. Put 'em on—— I don't care where you put 'em.

CHUB. *(Rising)* Wait! I have an idea.

Doc. This is too much. *(They look as if they were about to jump on him.)*

CHUB. Just a minute—— Restrain yourselves. Suppose we hang these—*(Indicating garments)* —in the clothes closet and leave the door slightly ajar. Then when G. P. comes in he will notice the—— *(Indicating negligee)* —you know—the toute ensemble—and we can say your wife had gone shopping before his telegram arrived. (STOKES *and* DOC *look at each other.* BOTH *are forced to a reluctant approval.)*

STOKES. What do you think?

Doc. *(Crossing* C. *to* R. *of* STOKES*)* Well, that's not so bad, eh?

CHUB. *(All confidence again, crosses to couch)* Sure—some day you will realize how brilliant I am.

Doc. Now, don't get swell-headed just because we let you live.

CHUB. Well, now, Doc—confess. The scheme was all right—the presents came—but how was I to know your family were a flock of hard-boiled eggs? *(Business of picking up presents and in going drops the "Teddy" and bloomers.)*

STOKES. *(Handing him a piece)* Here, you dropped the toute ensemble.

Doc. *(Indicating the nightgown)* Stoksie—

wrinkle them up a bit so they'll look used—you know.

STOKES. Suppose G. P. decided to wait until your wife comes back from shopping? (*Doc stops apprehensively. Boys dump boxes and paper in closet.*)

CHUB. You forget he sails for Bermuda at five. Just get the present from him.

DOC. Yes, just get the present from him first— that's the trick.

CHUB. Is he as close as all that?

DOC. Close! He thinks alum is an explosive. His favorite author is the receiving teller at the Bank. Why, the *Wall Street Journal* is his idea of a yellow sheet and to him the most thrilling love story of the ages is Smith's *Wealth of Nations.*

*(There is a CRASH off stage, preceded and followed by auto HORNS and EXPLOSIONS. ALL rush to L. window.)*

STOKES. By George! That is a mixup.

CHUB. That fellow in the touring car was on the wrong side of the street.

STOKES. There's a woman in the taxi—— Looks like she's hurt.

DOC. Hurry up—— They might take her to the doctor across the street and I need—I mean—I'm a much better doctor than he is. (*Pushes CHUB and STOKES out of door L.*)

STOKES. (*As he is going out*) Yes, and she has a good case against that touring car. I'll take care of that.

DOC. (*Jumping about unconsciously, glad and unable to suppress his excitement*) Somebody's hurt! Somebody's hurt! (*Rushing to medical cabinet*) My first patient. (*He fumbles with instruments and knocks them all over floor*) Gee, I'm nervous.

*(Enter STOKES and CHUB, carrying MARY, her face covered, followed by CLEM and MRS. MERRIVALE, who walks in without her cane.)*

MRS. MERRIVALE. Is she dead? Is she dead? *(STOKES and CHUB attempt to put MARY on couch. As her feet touch ground she moans with pain. MARY's stocking is torn and her ankle discolored with grease paint.)*

DOC. *(Kneeling at foot of couch)* It's her ankle.

CHUB. *(At couch. STOKES R. of couch. MRS. MERRIVALE and CLEM nearby)* Is she badly hurt?

CLEM. Shall I run for a doctor?

DOC. Doctor—— What do you mean?

MRS. MERRIVALE. I'll bet she's dead. I'll bet she's dead.

CHUB. *(To her)* What odds will you lay me?

STOKES. Cut it out, Chub. *(Crosses up. To DOC)* I'll be back in a minute. I want to get the taxi driver's name and the number of the big car.

DOC. *(Taking off MARY's shoe and stocking)* Here, you, help me!

STOKES. But I want to make a success of my first case. *(Exits L.)*

DOC. So do I. Chub, get me those bandages on the shelf. *(CHUB runs. To CLEM)* Get me that little black bag. *(CLEM runs for it.)*

MRS. MERRIVALE. *(Repeats DOC's orders and rushes aimlessly backward and forward)* Is she dead?

DOC. *(Is very commanding. To CHUB)* Tear off that bag and give me the bandages. *(To CLEM)* Open the bandages and give me the bottles.

CLEM. *(Opens bag and takes out empty beer bottle)* This?

DOC. *(Mechanically takes it and then hurriedly hides it under couch)* No, the other one.

CLEM. My Gawd, Maw, you forgot your cane.

MRS. MERRIVALE. *(Promptly faints as she realizes she is getting about without cane)* My cane! And I can't walk a step without it.

CLEM. *(Real panic whenever her mother pulls a faint)* Doctor! Look! Maw fainted. *(Doc drops MARY's ankle and rushes to MRS. MERRIVALE. Feels in grip for medicine; runs back to MARY. CHUB starts to bandage MARY's ankle.)*

CLEM. Take care of Maw first. *(Doc grabs bandages and hesitates where to go. In confusion kneels and starts to bandage MRS. MERRIVALE's ankle.)* Doctor Hampton, how dare you?

DOC. *(Is terribly embarrassed when he realizes what he has done. MRS. MERRIVALE revives and is assisted from room by CHUB and CLEM as STOKES enters L., writing in notebook.)* Take your mother downstairs—I'm losing my head.

MRS. MERRIVALE. *(Suddenly as she gets to door)* Is she dead?

CHUB. Not yet. But the Doc's working on her. *(MRS. MERRIVALE, CLEM and CHUB exit L., all ad libing.)*

STOKES. *(Comes L. of desk)* What's wrong?

DOC. I don't know whether it's broken or just badly sprained. Get me my small case. I want to have something ready to relieve the pain. *(STOKES gets case from cabinet.)* How about the fellow in the big car?

STOKES. Oh, he's all right—scratched up a bit—but no chance for you. The policeman has him in charge. My client has a great case. *(Very important about it.)*

DOC. *(Equally as important)* You mean my patient?

CHUB. *(Enters. Happy)* Some day! Eh, Doc?

DOC. A patient at last!

STOKES. A client at last!

CHUB. She's got on some swell scenery, too.

(MARY *moves slightly. Doc puts hand under her head and moves back her hat.*)

DOC. (*Dropping her head on pillow. He is all excitement*) Boys—look—I've found her!

CHUB. The Tag Day girl!

STOKES. Here's where we get our money back.

DOC. Money! You talk about *money* at a time like this? I wouldn't insult her.

CHUB. Doc—be reasonable.

STOKES. Yes, and it's a long time till Saturday night.

MARY. (*Trying to sit up. Doc helps her*) I must get there in time. (*As she opens her eyes.*)

DOC. It's all right. Don't excite yourself.

MARY. I must get there. The boat sails at five.

DOC. My God—how did she know?

MARY. What place is this and who are you?

DOC. (*Distinctly surprised and hurt*) Don't you remember me?

CHUB. That's your physician, Doctor Hampton.

MARY. My physician? What's the matter with me? (*Remembers*) Oh! Now I remember. Am I badly hurt, Doctor?

DOC. (*In most professional tones*) Well—er—perhaps rather severely—but not dangerously. It's your—(*Looks down and giggles*)—ankle.

MARY. (*Looks down and sees her bare ankle and tries to hide it. Winces in pain*) Oh, dear!

DOC. (*Gets pillow on which to rest ankle*) There—that feels better, doesn't it?

MARY. (*Smiling very sweetly up into his face*) Very much better, thank you—you're so kind.

DOC. (*A little flustered. To STOKES*) She's a dream. (*In his embarrassment puts MARY's stocking in his handkerchief pocket*) Excuse me—I'll be back in a moment—I want to take some medicine to one of my patients. (*Exits L. with large bottle of pills.*)

STOKES. *(Asserting himself)* Now, Madame, I want you to know that—er—we have a wonderful case.

MARY. Good Heavens! A case of what?

STOKES. Why—of damages.

MARY. Have we—— I beg your pardon, but who are you?

STOKES. Why, I'm your attorney.

MARY. My—you must pardon me—it must be the accident, but I don't remember—— Still, you all do seem very familiar.

CHUB. Sure, don't you remember the three dol— the three fellows on Tag Day?

MARY. *(Smiling in reminiscence)* Oh, of course I do. The doctor, the lawyer and the merchant chief. How silly of me to forget!

CHUB. *(Feeling in his pocket)* I couldn't—forget you.

STOKES. Why, yes, we have a wonderful case. You see, the other car was going way beyond the speed limit and was on the wrong side of the street——

CHUB. We could see that from the window——

STOKES. And as you were proceeding in an orderly and lawful manner, you are entitled to just and lawful damages. *(Enter DOC L. He is surprised at STOKES' progress with MARY.)* Now you just leave it in my hands and I—— *(During this speech, Doc does everything possible to attract MARY's attention, but STOKES manages by his swift speech and professional manner to hold her attention.)*

MARY. Oh! I will—I'll leave everything in your hands—I'm sure you're very capable.

STOKES. *(Swelling up)* Thank you. Your confidence greatly affects me.

MARY. But I'm afraid that I'm in no condition now to talk damages.

DOC. *(Who has been chafing under STOKES'*

*monopoly of* MARY's *attention, squeezes in* R. *of*
MARY) Certainly not. As your physician I posi-
tively refuse to have you agitated. *(Pushes* STOKES
*away and hisses)* Traitor! *(Bends over* MARY *and
is all attention.)*

MARY. *(Suddenly remembering)* What time is
it? *(None of the* BOYS *have watches.)*

CHUB. *(Looks out of the window and apparently
sees the time and announces—)* Four o'clock.

STOKES. It's just four o'clock.⎱  *(Repeating*
DOC. It's four o'clock.        ⎰   *together)*

CHUB. Just four. *(Speaking with* DOC *and*
STOKES. *They* ALL *glare at each other.)*

MARY. You must get me to the boat immediately.
I'm sailing for Bermuda at five.

DOC. *(Gazing at* STOKES) You're sailing for
Berhooda? What did you say?

MARY. I'm sailing for Bermuda at five.

DOC. *(Goes to desk. Picks up telegram; reads
aloud)* "Sailing on Bermudian at five." *(Turns to*
MARY) At what time?

MARY. At five.

CHUB. On what boat?

MARY. On the Bermudian.

DOC. *(Points to telegram as he glances at* CHUB
*and* STOKES, *excited)* But my dear young lady, it's
quite impossible—you won't be able to get about
for several days, at least.

MARY. But I must go—my aunt is waiting for me
at the boat.

DOC. But you need to be absolutely quiet.

MARY. I can be quiet on board ship.

CHUB. But you need constant—medical attention.

DOC. *(Shakes* CHUB's *hand gratefully)* For
several days—until Saturday, at least.

STOKES. Saturday!

MARY. *(Dejectedly)* But I can't spoil Aunt's
trip. Of course I know our private affairs don't

interest you—but it's very romantic. I wouldn't spoil it for a dozen sprained ankles. She has promised to meet an old sweetheart on board and they're to patch up a quarrel that separated them twenty years ago. Auntie is a widow now—and if I don't go she won't go—and—it will spoil everything.

Doc. But *your health* is the first consideration.

Mary. *(With an air of finality)* But I'm quite all right, I assure you. I wonder if I could ask a great service of the merchant chief.

Chub. Of me? *(Gloats over* Doc *and* Stokes; *crosses to her)* My life—if you wish it.

Doc. *(Sarcastically)* She said a *service*.

Mary. I'm afraid if I'm carried to the boat with my ankle bandaged up, it may give my Aunt a dreadful shock.

Chub. I'm sure it would give the whole ship a shock to see that wonderful ankle—a delightful shock.

Mary. You mustn't say things like that——

Chub. How can I help it——

Mary. Will you go to the boat and break the news gently to my Aunt? Say there has been an accident, but it isn't serious, and that I'll be there presently and for her please not to worry. Oh! I'm sure you know what to say—I'll just leave it to your good judgment.

Chub. *(Realizes she is sending him away)* Yes —of course—if you want me to go—I'll go—I much rather stay here——

Mary. And then I shall see you at the boat to thank you.

Chub. *(Realizing he will see her again)* That's right—so you will—I'll see you off.

Mary. My aunt's name is Mrs. Burns.

Chub. Mrs. Burns—I'll not forget that—I'll think of a ten cent cigar. Goodbye, boys—goodbye. I'll come back after I've seen the ship sail and tell you—just—how things are. *(Puts on hat pompously and goes to door. To* MARY*)* Your discrimination greatly affects me. *(Imitating* STOKES.*)*

MARY. You don't mind going, do you?

CHUB. Mind! I think it's a great idea. *(Exits* L. *with triumphant look at the* BOYS.*)*

MARY. *(She is very much amazed)* And now you will call a taxi and have me taken to the boat, won't you, Doctor?

DOC. When such a beautiful lady commands— what can I do but obey?

STOKES. Say, where do you get that stuff?

DOC. Stokes, will you be kind enough to go downstairs and ring for a taxi?

STOKES. What!—er—don't you think—considering the fact that I'm a stranger in this house—that it would be better if you went down. The landlady might object.

DOC. Not at all—not at all!

MARY. If you will—please, Mr. Attorney—I'd be so grateful.

STOKES. *(Melting under her gaze, assumes courtly air)* Anything for you—your slightest wish is my command. *(Bows low.)*

DOC. Sir Walter Raleigh, tell him to have it here immediately. *(Exit* STOKES L. MARY *laughs with* DOC *as soon as door closes.)* I'm sorry you're going away.

MARY. *(Coquettishly)* Why?

DOC. *(Confused)* Why—because I'm sorry to lose your case!—no, no!

MARY. Oh—I thought you meant something else.

DOC. *(Eagerly; sits on couch)* I did mean something else—I mean so much else I can't begin.

MARY. Well, don't try.

DOC. Didn't you really remember me at first?

MARY. I'm afraid not.

Doc. Aw—please—please remember me—or say you did, anyway.

MARY. Well, of course, the accident dazed me for a few moments, or I'm sure I would have remembered. *(Hand on arm.)*

Doc. I would have known you if I were unconscious. I haven't stopped thinking of you for one minute ever since that day you were here. Look— *(Points to flag in lapel of coat)* I'm still all decorated up. I made a vow that no other hands but yours would touch this flag.

MARY. How thrilling! But suppose we had never met again?

Doc. Then I should have gone to the grave with this over my heart! (MARY *laughs.)* But I knew we would meet again.

MARY. Perhaps we never would have if it hadn't been for that accident.

Doc. God bless that accident.

MARY. What a dreadful thing to say!

Doc. Not for a doctor.

MARY. But you don't even know my name.

Doc. I'm not going to let you get away this time without knowing your name—— *(Rises)* I've suffered enough the last ten days.

MARY. Doctor Hampton, are you trying to make love to me?

Doc. *(Takes hand; sits)* With all my heart and soul.

MARY. But you have only seen me once.

Doc. How can you say that? I've seen you a million times since Tag Day. Every moment of the day I see your face before me.

MARY. That must be awful.

Doc. It's wonderful! But that isn't the worst— you haunt me at night. You know you shouldn't do that—unless you are serious.

MARY. I shouldn't do what? Do you think that

just because I came in here on Tag Day and accepted some money from you——

Doc. Please don't speak of money at a time like this. *(Abruptly rises; crosses* C.) I suppose you live in a wonderful big house?

Mary. What has that to do with it?

Doc. You wouldn't live in a bungalow, would you? (Mary *laughs.*) Don't laugh at me.

Mary. You *are* the funniest man.

Doc. *(Crosses to her)* Will you let me call on you when you return from Bermuda?

Mary. But I hardly know you.

Doc. I can fix that up all right, if you will let me call. Will you? Quick—please—he's coming back. *(He takes her hand.)*

Mary. I will.

Doc. *(Kisses her hand)* Thank you.

Stokes. *(Comes in quickly and sees* Doc *kissing* Mary's *hand. Sarcastically)* Some doctor you are!

Doc. *(Pretends to have been taking pulse)* Ninety-eight—normal! (Mary *laughs.*)

Stokes. The taxi will be here in a moment. *(Elaborately to* Mary.)

Mary. I must settle my bill before the taxi comes and now—— (Doc *and* Stokes *both show renewed interest in life.)*

Doc. Oh, any time will do.

Mary. Oh, no, I must do it now. How much is it, Doctor?

Doc. Why, the usual thing. (Stokes *stands behind* Mary *and makes violent motions with his hands to indicate five dollars.)*

Mary. But doctors have different fees, haven't they? (Stokes *renews his signals.)*

Doc. *(With effort)* Yes, different doctors have different fees. Well, my usual fee—that is—if I ever had—I mean when I—well, my usual fee is—

five—but in your case—— (Stokes *is frantic with disgust.*)

Mary. I wouldn't think of allowing you to reduce your fee for me—no, indeed! (Stokes *and* Doc *look greatly relieved.* Mary *searches for her bag. She cannot find it*) Why, where is my purse? *(They* All *search for it.)* Oh, dear, I must have lost it in the accident. (Doc *and* Stokes *collapse.)*

Stokes. Why, that's outrageous. Was there anything valuable in it?

Mary. Well, the bag itself was very valuable—and I did have quite a bit of money. You see, I gave a luncheon to several friends—girl friends—*(To* Doc*)* —and was hurrying to meet my aunt at the boat. I feel so embarrassed.

Doc. Why, it's perfectly all right, I assure you.

Mary. You must send the bill to my father immediately.

Stokes. Where does he live?

Mary. In Elizabeth, New Jersey.

Doc. How long does it take to get a letter from Elizabeth, New Jersey?

Mary. Oh, you ought easily to have an answer by—Saturday.

Doc. Thank you. *(Shakes her hand, greatly relieved.)*

Mary. So you'll surely send it, won't you?

Doc. I'll take it over myself. *(Crossing* r.; *realizes what he is saying.* Stokes *coughs.)* In that way I can make your father's acquaintance and ask his permission to call on you.

Stokes. I think I'd better talk to your father about—the case, too.

Mary. That will be splendid.

Doc. *(At desk)* What is your favorite name and address—— I mean, what is your father's name and address?

Mary. Oh, it's a very common name.

STOKES. I can scarcely believe that.

MARY. Oh, it is, I assure you.

DOC. Let us judge of that.

MARY. Well, it's Smith—John Smith. (DOCTOR *and* STOKES *collapse.*) And the address is twenty-two hundred Main Street, Elizabeth, New Jersey. (STOKES *grabs the tail of* DOC's *coat.*)

DOC. (*Stuttering*) Repeat that, please—my friend interrupted me.

MARY. John Smith, twenty-two hundred Main Street, Elizabeth, and my name is commoner still—

DOC. Don't tell me it's Mary Jane.

MARY. (*Rising to her knees on couch. In great surprise*) How did you know?

DOC. (*Falling against chair, almost into* STOKES' *lap*) Oh, my God!

STOKES. (*Picking up wedding invitation from desk, reads*) "Mr. and Mrs. John Smith, twenty-two hundred Main Street, request pleasure—— Mary Jane Smith."

DOC. (*Repeats in daze*) Mary Jane Smith.

MARY. (*Hurt*) I knew it was a very common name, but I didn't think it was as bad as that.

DOC. (*Nervously tearing off pages from a note pad. They fall to floor*) My dear lady, don't think for one moment I am—— It's just peculiar—just extraordinary—— (*To* STOKES) Say something—

STOKES. It certainly was a great scheme.

MARY. I'm afraid I don't understand. (*DOOR-BELL rings.*) No doubt, that's my taxi. Will you see? (STOKES *this time vies with* DOC *to see if it is the taxi.*)

DOC. Why, certainly!

STOKES. Let me see! (*Reaches door first*) As I was allowed—(*Sarcastically*) —to ring for the taxi, I think I should be permitted the privilege of seeing if it has arrived.

DOC. (*Trying to sneak out of door*) Mary Jane

Smith—Mary Jane—— *(Stands like a man in a trance.)*

MARY. *(Becomes angry)* Doctor Hampton— (Doc *comes down.)* —you don't seem nearly as pleased to be left alone with me as you were a moment ago, and I want to take back my promise to let you call.

DOC. Oh, Miss Smith—— *(Almost chokes on the name.)*

MARY. If the mere mention of a name affects you so, I——

DOC. What's in a name? (STOKES *enters, very much agitated. Calls* Doc *to him and speaks in whisper.)*

STOKES. It's your uncle, G. P.

DOC. Oh, Lord!

STOKES. He wants to meet your wife.

DOC. *(Taking* STOKES R. *to desk)* Wait a minute. *(Looks at* MARY; *whispers to* STOKES*)* Follow my lead. *(Aloud.* STOKES *at* L. *of desk.* DOC C.*)* Yes. You say the patient insists on seeing me?

STOKES. Yes, Doctor.

DOC. But didn't you explain to him that I had another patient here?

STOKES. *(Uneasily)* I did, Doctor.

DOC. *(Very professionally)* Well—perhaps I can make Miss Smith understand. You see, Miss Smith —I am a specialist—not an ankle specialist—as you might suppose——

STOKES. Oh, no—no——

DOC. But a brain specialist.

STOKES. Yes, indeed!

DOC. Perhaps it will be unnecessary for me to explain to you that there are a great many people in this world who suffer from one delusion and one only. Otherwise they are quite normal. Isn't that so, Stokes?

STOKES. Yes, indeed. Yes, indeed.

MARY. Really?

Doc. For example. Stokes here suffers under the delusion that he's a lawyer.

STOKES. Yes, indeed! *(Says it enthusiastically; realizes his mistake; glares at* Doc.*)*

Doc. And a great many so-called crazy people think they are some celebrated man, like—Napoleon. Apart from that one belief they are thoroughly normal. Isn't that so, Stoksie?

STOKES. Yes, indeed! *(Grouchily.)*

MARY. How interesting!

Doc. It is! Very! *(Tries to be casual)* I have one patient who imagines that everyone he sees—it's ridiculous, I know—he imagines everyone he sees has just been married, and goes about congratulating people. It's very embarrassing at times. *(*STOKES *is dumfounded.)*

MARY. I should think it would be.

Doc. He is downstairs now.

MARY. Oh, Heavens—don't bring him in here. I should be terrified. I'm frightened to death at crazy people.

Doc. But he's only crazy on one subject and if you don't disagree with him he's quite harmless.

MARY. I'm terribly nervous, but if you say it's all right——

STOKES. I will be here to protect you.

Doc. *(Rises)* That's not necessary at all. Ask him to come up. *(*STOKES *exits* L.*)* Now—he—he's liable to think I'm married or that you're married—of course you are not married, are you?

MARY. Certainly not.

Doc. Fine! Neither am I. *(Laughs foolishly and then catches himself)* And if by any chance he should speak to you and congratulate you—just humor him along and don't for a moment let him think it is anything strange or unnatural, will you?

MARY. But I'm in no condition to see a crazy man.

Doc. *(Drops on knees by couch; grabs her hand)* Please, I never asked you to do me a favor in all my life before.

MARY. Of course you haven't—— Why should you?

Doc. Please do this—— It's very vital to me. I'll explain some time—— Won't you?

MARY. Well, I'll try—but I do wish my taxi was here.

Doc. You will be doing me a great favor.

MARY. Then I will.

*(Enter STOKES, followed by G. P. HAMPTON, who enters with a rush. He has grip in his hand. G. P. stops C.)*

Doc. This is an unexpected pleasure.

G. P. Is it? *(Goes to chair L. of desk; puts down coat.)*

Doc. Indeed it is.

G. P. Before I congratulate you, I want to see your wife. *(MARY is on her knees on couch and backs up gradually. She is frightened of G. P., as she thinks he is crazy.)*

Doc. Oh, my wife. *(Makes motion to MARY. G. P. looks her over very critically, grins and says, "Ah!" MARY becomes uneasy and turns to Doc for protection. He takes her hand soothingly. MARY evidently meets with G. P.'s approval, for his face gradually breaks into smiles. EVERYONE is much relieved, from entirely different motives. G. P. shakes Doc's hand.)*

G. P. My boy! My boy! I do congratulate you! It's the first sensible thing you ever did. *(To STOKES)* By George, he's some picker, eh? And I suppose, my dear, I'll have to congratulate you, too.

MARY. *(Shrinks away, frightened)* That isn't necessary.

G. P. *(To* MARY*)* You mustn't mind my abrupt, blunt way—but I was pretty anxious to see just what kind of a girl that young scamp had married. *(Turns* R.*)*

MARY. *(To* DOC*)* Don't leave me.

DOC. I'm *with* you.

G. P. I was afraid this young man had made a mess of things. It didn't look just right to me.

DOC. You hurt me, sir!

G. P. *(Laughing)* I can tell you this now that I've seen your wife. Your old uncle is proud of you. *(Slaps* DOC *on back; turns to* STOKES, *who tries to smile but is frightened.)*

MARY. *(To* DOC*)* Uncle! *(*DOC *points to forehead to indicate* G. P. *is crazy.)*

G. P. Yes, sir, if I'm any judge of character, you're a fine girl. *(*MARY, *in her eagerness to get away from* G. P., *has worked to head of couch, with* DOC *supporting her.* G. P. *holds out his hand to her.* MARY *timidly gives hers to him.* G. P. *shakes it vigorously.)*

MARY. *(Very much puzzled)* I thank you—— Excuse my not getting up, but I've sprained my ankle.

G. P. I'm so sorry to hear that, just as you're married. At any rate—*(*MARY *moves away in alarm)* —I want to say I'm proud to welcome you into the family.

MARY. *(Gazing straight out)* Family?

G. P. You know, I haven't been any too generous with the young scamp.

DOC. Oh, sir! You wrong yourself.

G. P. *(Turning to* MARY*)* No, no, don't pretend. But the world seems kind of different today, and when I look at you two fine, healthy young people happily married, starting out in life together with

each other's love to help you on, well—I see I've
missed a lot. It's a great mistake to just make
money and hoard it up.

MARY. He doesn't seem crazy.

DOC. Not when he talks like that.

G. P. I like you—I like everything about you—
your looks—your sweetness—and I like your name,
Mary.

MARY. Mary! Why, how did he know?

STOKES. I'll go for the taxi.

DOC. *(Pulling him back by his coat tails)* No,
no! You coward!

G. P. Who is that young fellow?

DOC. Why—he's my—her—our attorney——

G. P. Attorney? You're not getting ready for a
divorce already?

DOC. *(Trying to laugh)* Yes—no—I should say
not—not yet, are we, Mary?

MARY. *(Again rising on her knees)* No—no—not
yet! Pardon me, but how did you know my name
was Mary?

DOC. Ssh—mum—tut, tut.

G. P. You forget it was on the invitation, my
dear.

MARY. Invitation? What invitation?

G. P. The wedding invitation. I was in Chicago
when it arrived. That's why you haven't heard from
me before. Let's see, where did I put that——
*(Fumbles in his pockets of coat on chair L. of desk.)*

DOC. It's all right—— Don't bother—don't
bother, Uncle.

MARY. *(Suspiciously)* Then he is your uncle.

DOC. Why—er—kind of an uncle.

MARY. What kind?

G. P. Ah, here it is.

MARY. May I see the invitation?

G. P. Certainly, my dear. It's the same as the
rest of the family received. *(Hands her invitation)*

And now—since you've settled down with a fine, charming girl like Mary, I'm going to fix you up right—car, swell office, and by George! I'll buy you the finest bunch of knives and scissors of any doctor in town. Of course, it depends on whether you treat her right or not. So you see, Mary, the young rascal's future is in your hands.

Doc. It certainly is.

Mary. *(Reads invitation)* Oh! Oh! *(Keeps saying "Oh!" First she is furious. When Doc keeps saying, "Oh, please!" she gradually melts with her "Ohs" and becomes less angry.)*

G. P. *(Sees Mary excited over invitation)* What's the matter, Mary?

Doc. *(To Mary)* I'm in your hands. Oh, please!

G. P. What's the matter, Mary?

Mary. My—my ankle. (Doc *and* Stokes *are relieved.)*

Doc. You must excuse Mary. She's very nervous and she has just sprained her uncle—ankle.

G. P. Mary does look a bit pale and nervous. What she needs is a sea voyage.

Mary. Indeed, I do.

Doc. But, Uncle—we—we couldn't afford it.

G. P. You leave that to me—— By George, that will be my wedding present.

Stokes. Good night!

G. P. You must come with me today. I'm sailing at five o'clock this afternoon on "The Bermudian" for Bermuda.

Mary. There's something strange about this.

Doc. We couldn't get ready in that time, could we, Mary.

Mary. *(Maliciously)* I could!

Doc. But my large practice. (Stokes *coughs violently.)* This is so sudden.

G. P. Well, so was your marriage. It's the only way to take a trip—make up your mind quick.

You enjoy it more. Besides, you haven't had a
honeymoon yet, have you?

Doc. *(Barely glancing at* MARY*)* N—no.

G. P. Just take a grip and throw in some of those
pretties hanging up in the closet there. *(*MARY
*looks and starts violently.)* This young man will
show me where the phone is and I'll engage accommodations for two. *(*STOKES *grabs his hat, glad to
get out.* G. P. *crosses to door)* And my boy, I'm
going to give you a nice, substantial check, too.

Doc. Check?

G. P. I haven't the time to make it out *now*. I'll
give it to you on the boat. *(Exits* L. *with* STOKES.*)*

MARY. *(Turning fiercely on* Doc*)* Doctor Hampton—how dare you use my name in this way?

Doc. *(Crossing to her)* It's all a mistake, Mary.

MARY. Mistake! Do you expect me to believe
that? Here it is in black and white—Mary Jane
Smith—Main Street, Elizabeth, New Jersey. It's
monstrous—I shall start a suit against you. Where's
my attorney? *(Turns around* L. *where* STOKES *was.)*

Doc. Please—please—— Wait until Uncle goes
and I promise I can explain everything.

MARY. Oh, if it weren't for this ankle.

Doc. *(Sits; takes her hand)* First of all, I want
to thank you for not giving me away. You're a
thoroughbred—and I love you for it.

MARY. We'll dispense with the compliments.
What about this invitation?

Doc. Those are fake invitations. I give you my
word of honor I had no idea there was a real person by that name. We took the commonest name we
could think of—— *(Stops; blunders)* You know
what I mean?

MARY. No, I don't know what you mean. *(Looks
at clothes in closet)* Whose clothes are these?

Doc. They're yours!

MARY. What! Doctor Hampton, I think you're the one that needs medical attention.

DOC. They are wedding presents sent by my dear relatives to Mary. I sent out some fake invitations because I was broke. You know that fellow Chub you sent down to the boat? Well, it was his idea—not mine. I thought they'd send something I could sell—or pawn. But not *my* relatives. (MARY *begins to laugh.*) You believe me? (MARY *laughs more.*) Really? Then you're not angry with me. I can face anything if you're not angry with me.

MARY. *(Laughing)* Angry! I'm furious—but—that's all they sent for wedding gifts? It's too funny. I'm just thinking what will happen on the boat.

DOC. Believe me—there ain't going to be no boat. *(Enter G. P. Doc goes to R.C.)*

G. P. Listen. Listen to the good news. I was able to get the bridal suite for you. (Doc *backs into closet.* MARY *feigns collapse.*)

MARY. Oh!

G. P. *(Shyly)* And my boy—I've engaged the bridal suite for the return trip—for myself and bride.

DOC. *(To MARY)* I told you he was crazy.

G. P. You two young lovers needn't think you have the monopoly on happiness—that's really why I came East—to meet an old sweetheart of mine. We quarrelled twenty years ago—and she married another man. But I'm going to meet her on the boat, and if she'll have me this time, why——

MARY. Why—what's her name?

G. P. Her name is Mrs. Burns.

MARY. And what is your name? G. P. Hampton from Fargo? And did you live in Buffalo—years ago?

G. P. How did you know? Oh, of course, George has been telling you.

MARY. Yes, George has been telling me a lot.

G. P. It's funny, but her name was Mary Jane Smith, too. But of course Smith is such a common name.

Doc. Of course. It's too common, that's the whole trouble.

Mary. Yes!

G. P. It's just one of those little coincidences.

Mary. It certainly is one of those little coincidences. She's my aunt.

G. P. Your aunt! Isn't that splendid? *(Goes to Doc; shakes his hand.)*

Doc. Isn't it? Isn't it just splendid?

G. P. Bless my heart! Your aunt. Just think—your aunt!

Doc. Yes, just think!

G. P. *(Still shaking Doc's hand)* Couldn't be better—could it? Just couldn't be better.

Doc. No, it couldn't possibly be better.

G. P. Because now Mary can help me plead my case with her aunt. I confess I'm very nervous. *(To Mary)* Tell me, how does she look?

Mary. Auntie has changed a bit—you may not remember her.

G. P. Not remember her? Why, I'd know her in a million. Of course, she may not know me. I've grown—well, I haven't the figure I used to have. I'm afraid she'll be too disappointed to have me. That's the reason why I want you two as my allies.

Doc. I'm afraid I wouldn't have much influence, sir.

G. P. But Mary wouldn't go without you.

Mary. Oh, yes, I would.

G. P. I wouldn't think of separating you two young lovers.

Mary. But really I don't mind.

G. P. Oh, yes, you do. There has been a little tiff. I saw from the first that there was something wrong.

Doc. *(Scared)* You did?

G. P. But we'll straighten out everything at the boat.

Doc. Really, sir—I can't go.

G. P. Listen, my boy—we have less than one hour to pack up and catch that boat.

Doc. But if you only knew.

G. P. I only know I can't miss that boat. *(KNOCKING on door.)*

Doc. Come in.

Clem. *(Standing at door)* For Gawd's sake, Doctor Hampton, will you get Pollyanna home? Maw's driving me crazy.

Doc. *(With conviction as he shakes G. P.'s hand)* That settles it—Uncle, I'll go.

G. P. Of course you will. Here, young woman. You pack up those doo-dads in the closet there. *(Crosses to door.)*

Clem. *(Looks in closet)* What! *(Examines them; sees wrinkles)* Um—hum—that's very strange.

G. P. Strange—strange—— What's strange about it?

Clem. What's strange about it? Say, you're as bad as he is.

G. P. Come, my good girl—hurry, pack those things. *(Gives her bill. At first she is indignant; then she looks at money, puts it in her apron pocket and begins to pack bag.)* I'll slip downstairs a moment. I must 'phone my bank and one or two other places. I'll expect you to be ready when I come back. *(Exits L.)*

Clem. Do you want me to pack all these things, Miss—Mrs.—I don't know what you are.

Mary. You needn't bother. *(Turns to Clem, who recognizes her for the first time and is delighted to see her again.)*

Doc. *(To Mary)* I'm afraid I can't go.

MARY. But your uncle has the bridal suite for you.

Doc. What?

MARY. And Auntie and I have our stateroom.

CLEM. *(Holding up nightie and pajama suit)* Do you want these in?

Doc. Certainly.

MARY. Certainly not.

CLEM. Well, am I going to pack it, or am I not?

Doc. Do as you are told and ask no questions.

CLEM. There's lots of questions could be askt if you askt me. Do you want all these in or just one set? *(Holding up underwear.)*

MARY. Oh, please be quiet.

CLEM. Well, I was only askin'.

MARY. Oh! One will do.

CLEM. Then you ain't goin' to be gone long?

MARY. Yes, quite some time.

CLEM. And you only want one set? Oh, of course it ain't none of my business.

MARY. Really, Doctor, I can't have this.

CLEM. *(Slamming grip)* There you are. It makes no difference to me if you don't take nothin' with you. *(Exits grandly L.)*

MARY. What will she think of me?

Doc. What could she think of you except that you're the sweetest, most charming——

MARY. You're not timid in every way, are you?

STOKES. *(Enters; crossing L. of couch)* My Lord, the taxi ticks.

MARY. Your uncle engaged accommodations for two. Why not take our attorney along—you may need him.

STOKES. Where are you going—to jail?

Doc. No, I'm going crazy. G. P. has engaged accommodations for Bermuda for two. What do you say, Stokes?

STOKES. I'm in favor of going any place until Saturday night.

MARY. He said he would give you a check—on the boat.

STOKES. Then we'll go on the boat.

DOC. I can't face the music.

STOKES. Looks like there's a band at both ends, Doc.

G. P. *(Enters)* I told the landlady you'd be giving up your room. She seemed very much put out about it.

*(MRS. MERRIVALE and CLEM enter excitedly.)*

MRS. MERRIVALE. It isn't true you're going away, is it, Doctor? Tell me it isn't true. *(Takes his arm.)*                    *(WARN Curtain.)*

DOC. I'm afraid it is.

G. P. Come! Come! I'll have no more quibbling.

MRS. MERRIVALE. I'm not quibbling—I'm a sick woman and I need him.

G. P. I told you not to take up medicine. Come on, everybody.

MARY. How will I get downstairs? I can't walk.

STOKES. Let's make a hand basket like we used to do when we were kids. *(They do so. MARY gets on hand basket.)*

MRS. MERRIVALE. *(Shrieks)* What about *Polly-anna?*

DOC. There's a ticket in an envelope on the desk. You'll find Pollyanna at that address.

MRS. MERRIVALE. What place is it, a hospital?

DOC. Kind of a hospital, if you look at it that way.

CLEM. If you look at it that way? *(Doc and STOKES are gradually backing off with MARY.)*

DOC. If you need any money for her, I'll send it to you along with some nice onions.

CLEM. Onions! Where are you going?

Doc. To Bermuda. (MRS. MERRIVALE *screams.*)

CLEM. What for?

Doc. My honeymoon.

MARY. *(Boxing his ear)* He is not. *(They exit.)*

MRS. MERRIVALE. What's to become of my poor liver?

G. P. *(At the door)* Turn it over to some other doctor.

## CURTAIN

# ACT THREE

SCENE: *Deck of the Steamship Bermudian, contain-
ing the bridal suite, Stateroom Number Three
and the saloon, in New York harbor, with
ground row and rear showing New York skyline, skyscrapers, etc.*

    *Ground row is constructed so as to move on
a cue, giving effect of boat movement. Cyclo-
rama water drop in rear. Effect of clouds and
water.*

    CHUB *and* MRS. BURNS *are discovered talk-
ing as Curtain rises. They are standing on deck
of steamer, outside of Stateroom Number
Three.*

    STEWARD *enters* R.I. *He is rather effeminate.*

MRS. BURNS. *(To* STEWARD*)* What time is it?

STEWARD. It's five and twenty minutes of five.

MRS. BURNS. Will we leave on time?

STEWARD. As far as I know we will, ma'm. As
far as I know——— *(Exits* R.U. CHUB *imitates him
and laughs.)*

MRS. BURNS. *(To* CHUB*)* Are you quite sure it
is safe for her to make the trip?

CHUB. It is only a slight sprain—the doctor said
so.

MRS. BURNS. Has she a good doctor?

CHUB. He says he is. You ought to see the people in his office.

MRS. BURNS. I'll put on a wrap and then we'll go
to the gangplank and meet her. Excuse me just a
moment. *(She goes into stateroom.)*

G. P. *(Enters* R.U. *with* STEWARD*)* Is this the bridal suite? (CHUB *turns at mention of bridal suite.)*

STEWARD. Yes, sir.

G. P. Well, I want you to do the thing up right— understand? *(Gives him a bill.)*

STEWARD. *(Laughs)* Yes, indeed.

G. P. Spare no expense and do it quietly, as I want it to be a big surprise. (G. P. *goes into bridal suite; gives him another bill.* STEWARD *laughs again and this annoys* G. P.*)*

CHUB. *(To* STEWARD*)* Is that the bridegroom?

STEWARD. That? Oh, no, sir—the bridal couple are below. They're young 'uns.

CHUB. Gee! I'd like to see them. (STEWARD *goes into bridal suite and can be seen through windows taking orders from* G. P.*)*

MRS. BURNS. *(Entering from stateroom. She has hat on and purse in hand)* And now will you take me downstairs?

CHUB. With pleasure. *(As they near bridal suite)* Look, they're fixing up the bridal suite for some poor victims.

MRS. BURNS. Why do you say victims?

CHUB. Everybody calls people who are just married or just going to be married, victims—for fun.

MRS. BURNS. Well, I think it's rather cheap and vulgar fun.

CHUB. I can laugh because I'm not married. Is your niece?

MRS. BURNS. *(Abstracted)* My niece? Oh, no!

G. P. *(Comes out of door of bridal suite and almost bumps into* MRS. BURNS *as she passes)* I beg your pardon. *(He backs into bridal suite. She turns to look after him as she rounds deck.)*

MRS. BURNS. Who is that man? Do you know him?

CHUB. No, I don't know—— He has something

to do with the bridal party, I think—probably the father of the bride.

MRS. BURNS. Oh, I see—then it can't be—— *(They exit R.I.)*

G. P. *(To* STEWARD, *as they come out of bridal suite)* Who is that lady? *(Pointing in direction* MRS. BURNS *and* CHUB *have gone.)*

STEWARD. I don't know the name, sir. She and another lady have the stateroom next door.

G. P. She and another lady? Then it can't be— *(Gives him tip.* STEWARD *laughs again.)* Well, you attend to everything for me and do it as quickly and quietly as possible. (G. P. *exits* R.I. STEWARD *shuts door of bridal suite and starts to follow.)*

*(*MARY, STOKES *and* DOC *enter from* R.U. DOC *and* STOKES *are carrying* MARY *in hand-basket fashion as in Exit of Act II.)*

MARY. *(Looking behind)* Please hurry.

STEWARD. *(Looking on with surprise at* MARY's *ankle)* Shall I get you a wheel-chair, sir?

DOC. That's not a bad idea at all.

STEWARD. *(Hurrying off* R.I) Right away, sir. Poor thing, she's sprained her ankle.

MARY. Isn't it ridiculous the way people stare at anything out of the ordinary?

DOC. You can't blame the people for that. It's all I've done for an hour.

MARY. Oh, I'm not flattering myself they're looking at me.

STOKES. Well—they are in a way. *(Glances at ankle.)*

DOC. Stokes, eyes front. *(Commandingly.)*

MARY. *(Tries to hide her bare foot under her dress)* Crowds are the most ridiculous things, anyway. All one need do is something unusual and——

STOKES. Where have I heard that before?

Doc. I wonder where *he* is?

MARY. Who?

Doc. The Columbus of the wedding invitations.

MARY. Oh, yes—those wedding invitations! Please put me down. *(They do so.)*

Doc. Lean on me! }
STOKES. Lean on me! }  *(Together)*

MARY. Mr. Attorney, will you find out from the Purser just where my stateroom is?

STOKES. I'm afraid you can't stand alone.

Doc. Alone? Did you say alone?

MARY. I can stand on one foot—like a stork—if Doctor Hampton will support me.

Doc. Support you? I ask no more in life than that.

MARY. Please don't be silly.

STOKES. You don't know how silly it is.

Doc. Run along, Mr. Attorney, and find out where the lady's stateroom is.

MARY. Please do—because I want to be settled before my aunt sees me.

STOKES. I'll hurry right back.

Doc. Don't hurry on my account—I'm strong— (STOKES *exits* R.I) —for Mary.

MARY. This is the first chance I've had to be alone with you.

Doc. I know. Did you ever see such a bunch of glue merchants?

MARY. That isn't what I mean at all. I want to know exactly what you are going to do.

Doc. I know what I'd like to do. *(Leaning toward her as though he would kiss her. Starts to kiss her as* STEWARD *and* G. P. *are appearing on scene.* G. P. *nods head and motions to* STEWARD.*)*

G. P. Aren't they the loving couple? *(He exits* R.I.*)*

STEWARD. *(Coming forward and grinning foolishly)* Can I do anything for you?

Doc. Yes—you can jump overboard.

Steward. *(Smiling slyly)* Oh, I see.

Mary. You don't see at all.

Steward. *(Still smiling)* I promise not to see another thing. I didn't realize for the moment——

Mary. You didn't realize what?

Steward. Nothing—nothing at all.

Mary. You're quite ridiculous. We're—I'm merely looking for my stateroom.

Steward. It's right here, madam. *(Points to bridal suite.)*

Doc. Are you sure?

Steward. Yes, sir.

Mary. Will you help me there, please?

Doc. I'll carry you in. *(Picks her up and carries her.)*

Steward. That's very romantic, I'm sure. (Mary and Doc *glare at him.)*

Mary. I don't think this is my room. *(Inside door of bridal suite)* I don't see my bags here——

Steward. Yes, ma'm—that's the bridal suite.

Mary. *(Alarmed that someone might see her there)* The bridal suite?

Doc. That's my room!

Steward. Yes, sir—and if I may be allowed to say so—I wish you both much happiness. *(Exits* R.1 *with his funny laugh.)*

Mary. Take me out of here! Do you hear? Take me out of here. Take me out of here. What made that Steward think—what he thought?

Doc. I don't know. I didn't send him any invitation. Perhaps it was because I had my arm around your waist.

Mary. Then take your arm away at once.

Doc. You'll fall if I do.

Mary. I'll be compromised if you don't. (Doc *takes arm away and* Mary *totters.* Doc *walks to* L., Mary *hopping after him on one foot until they are at extreme* L., *then* Doc *steps back with her to bridal suite, humming as he does so.)*

Doc. See—you can't do without me. Only storks can stand that way successfully. Wonderful bird, the stork!

Mary. Who said anything about storks?

Doc. Why, you did.

Mary. I did not.

Doc. Now, Mary Jane, I heard you say it. Doctors and storks have a certain community of association.

Stokes. *(Enters* R.1 *hurriedly, carrying steamer chair, folded up. Out of breath)* Was I long?

Doc. You must have met yourself coming back.

Mary. Did you find the number of my stateroom?

Stokes. No. There was a long line in front of the Purser's window, so I brought this chair to make you comfortable in the meantime.

Doc. *(Sarcastically)* Now, wasn't that sweet of you!

Mary. *(Reproving* Doc*)* It was! Very considerate.

Doc. You arrange the chair and I will lift her in it. *(Lifts* Mary *up.)*

Stokes. *(Funny business opening steamer chair)* Shall I put it there?

Doc. No—I think over here. (Stokes *moves it.)*

Stokes. Here? *(During this scene* Doc *looks intently at* Mary *and pays no attention to* Stokes.*)*

Doc. No, I think your first suggestion was best.

Stokes. *(Fixing steamer rug)* Of course it was. There, now!

Doc. A little further over here.

Stokes. Oh—— *(Impatiently.)*

Doc. Now face this way.

Stokes. It *is* facing this way.

Doc. Then put it back again.

Stokes. What's the matter? Don't you like that?

*(Chair is finally placed in C. of space between bridal suite and tormenter.)*

Doc. I think it's wonderful. *(Looking at* Mary.*)*

Stokes. *(Looking up)* Say—what is this?

Doc. *(Turns to* Stokes, Mary *still in his arms)* Oh—yes, it's a steamer chair, isn't it?

Stokes. Pay a little attention to me, will you?

Doc. I'm paying as little as possible. *(Takes* Mary *to chair and puts her in it.)*

Stokes. And don't try any of your cheap comedy on me. What do you think I am?

Doc. I think you're a very good lawyer if you ever get a chance.

Stokes. *(To* Mary*)* Does the chair suit you?

Mary. Perfectly.

Stokes. *(Looking triumphantly at* Doc*)* Well, that's all I care about.

Mary. And now will you be good enough to find out the number of my stateroom? *(*Doc *laughs.* Mary *is sending* Stokes *away again.)*

Stokes. Certainly—right away.

Doc. And don't lose your place in the line this time. *(*Stokes *exits* R.I *and bumps into* Steward, *who is carrying basket of fruit.* Stokes *steals a piece.* Steward *also has huge bouquet of flowers. He smiles broadly at* Mary *and* Doc *and enters bridal suite.)*

Stokes. I beg pardon, Captain.

Mary. Why does he smile at us in that silly way? Tell him to stop it.

Doc. Well, I don't know whether I can stop a man from smiling.

Mary. That's the second time it's happened.

Doc. I'll speak to him. *(To* Steward*)* Steward, why did you smile in that peculiar way just now?

Steward. Did I smile in a peculiar way, sir?

Doc. You certainly did.

Steward. It's the only smile I've got, sir.

MARY. I'll complain to the Captain. Is there anything unusual about us? *(The* STEWARD *grins.)*

Doc. You hear what the lady says?

STEWARD. That's all right, sir—they're all bashful when they come on board.

Doc. They? All?

STEWARD. Yes, sir—they all try to hide it at first.

Doc. Well, understand this—I have nothing to hide.

STEWARD. *(Looking significantly at* Doc*)* I should say you haven't. I wouldn't hide her either. *(Exits* R.I.*)*

Doc. *(Following* STEWARD *a few steps)* Confound him!

MARY. How terrible! He thinks we're married, too. Go at once to the Purser and the Captain and tell them we're not married—tell the whole ship.

Doc. But I can't go about the ship saying "I'm not married—I'm not married!"

MARY. Well, stop them some way. I don't care how you do it. Hurry, do you hear? I won't have it. *(*Doc *exits* R.U. MARY *tries to rise, but finds she cannot.)*

CHUB. *(Enters from* R.I*)* Oh, there you are. How's the ankle?

MARY. Splendid, thank you. Where is my aunt?

CHUB. She's waiting for you at the gangplank. *(Bends attentively over* MARY *and takes her hand as* G. P. *comes around deck* R.U. *He looks surprised; shakes his head disapprovingly.* G. P. *is smoking cigar and emphasizes the following scene by puffing at it.)*

MARY. Was she worried about me?

CHUB. No, indeed—I fixed everything fine.

MARY. Thank you so much—I knew you would.

CHUB. Did you notice the expression on Doc's face when I left today?

MARY. No.

Chub. If looks could have killed, I would have been in the morgue an hour ago.

Mary. Really?

Chub. Yes. He's terribly jealous of me. (G. P. *is standing by door of bridal suite.*)

Mary. Is he?

Chub. I should say he is. But we don't care anything about him, do we?

Mary. No. We don't care anything about him. (G. P. *is puffing cigar.*)

Chub. May I call on you when you return from Bermuda?

Mary. We shall see—when I return from Bermuda. (G. P. *exits* R.I *with the attitude of fear for* Doc. Doc *and* Stokes *enter, unobserved. They hear* Chub *talking to* Mary *and listen. They enter from around deck* R.U. *and lean against bridal suite.*)

Chub. I hope you won't be gone long. *(Starts to go, but stops and laughs)* I was just thinking what a laugh I'd have on the boys when I get back.

Mary. Why?

Chub. Why? They'll pass away with envy because I'm the only one to see you off.

Mary. What makes you think the other boys won't come down to the boat?

Chub. Oh, I know they won't come down. They have very important business to transact with a man from the West. As a matter of fact, I should be with them now. They can't make a move without me.

Stokes *and* Doc. Yes?

Chub. *(Surprised)* Well, of all the nerve! Had to come down to the boat, didn't you?

Doc. We had to come, all right.

Stokes. It's a shame, Chub, for you to speak that way of us.

Doc. Yes, it cuts us to the quick.

Chub. You fellows haven't got a quick.

MARY. *(To* CHUB*)* Will you please tell my aunt I'm here?

STOKES. Run along, Chubby—run along.

CHUB. Don't talk to me in that superior manner. (CHUB *goes off* R.I *in a rage.* STOKES *keeps shooing him off.*)

MARY. *(To* STOKES*)* What is the number of my stateroom?

STOKES. It's number three.

MARY. I want to go to it. *(They* BOTH *offer to carry her. She motions them away)* I thought that Steward said he would bring a wheelchair immediately. I suppose if we had tipped him he would have found one quickly enough. (Boys *look at each other.*) Will you hurry it along, Mr. Attorney?

Doc. Yes—run along, Stoksie—run along.

(STOKES *backs away reluctantly, making motion to* Doc *that he has no money.*)

MARY. And Doctor Hampton—please see where stateroom Number Three is.

STOKES. *(Grinning maliciously)* Yes—run along, Doc—run along.

Doc. Don't you know where it is, Stokes?

STOKES. *(Looks at door and sees Number Three)* No, I haven't the faintest idea. I think it's on the other side of the boat. *(Exits* R.I.*)*

Doc. *(Looks up and sees Number Three)* Here is stateroom Number Three. You see, Fate decrees we shall not part.

MARY. Fate has nothing to do with this case, Doctor Hampton, and don't act frivolously with me. The only reason I didn't expose you this afternoon is because your uncle is going to marry my aunt and you are sort of in the family.

(CHUB *and* MRS. BURNS *come on together* R.I.)

CHUB. Here she is, Mrs. Burns.

MRS. BURNS. Oh, my dear child—how do you feel? How is your ankle?

MARY. *(Kisses* AUNT*)* It's only a slight sprain, Auntie, and it will be well in no time, won't it, Doctor?

DOC. *(Professionally)* With a little attention—I think we need have no fear. (CHUB *is* R. DOC L. *of* CHUB. MARY *in chair and* MRS. BURNS L. *of chair.)*

MRS. BURNS. *(Very much surprised)* Is this the doctor?

MARY. Oh, I beg your pardon, Auntie. This is Doctor——

MRS. BURNS. *(Interrupting her)* Is this really the Doctor?

CHUB. Oh, yes, he's a real doctor.

MRS. BURNS. Aren't you very young to be a doctor? This seems to be the age for young people.

CHUB. That's what I tell him.

DOC. Let's not discuss what you tell me. You know, Mrs. Burns, I've had the pleasure of meeting you before. *(Shows flag)* Don't you remember Tag Day?

MRS. BURNS. That's what this young man said.

DOC. He did. He seems to have been talking quite a lot—as usual. Don't mind my friend, Mrs. Burns—he's irresponsible. Suffers mental trouble.

MARY. Mental trouble again. *(Stops abruptly)* That reminds me—Mr. Merchant Chief—the doctor and I have something to tell my aunt—privately. Will you excuse us just a moment?

CHUB. Why, certainly, Miss Burns. (DOC *pushes* CHUB *off* R.I.)

MARY. Miss Burns! Did he say Miss Burns?

MRS. BURNS. What is the great secret?

MARY. Auntie—the doctor's name is Hampton.

MRS. BURNS. Hampton?

MARY. Yes, and he's a nephew of your Mr. Hampton.

MRS. BURNS. Really—you must be Andrew Hampton's son.

DOC. I am. Did you know my dad?

MRS. BURNS. Know him? Why, your father, your uncle and I grew up together, and what a harum-scarum, mischievous scamp your father was —always doing the most impossible things.

MARY. Do you believe in heredity, Doctor?

DOC. There's nothing to it at all. *(Anxious to change conversation)* How—how's the ankle?

MARY. It is scarcely swollen at all, see?

MRS. BURNS. Why, Mary—you don't mean to say you came through the streets with your foot bare?

MARY. I'm afraid I did.

DOC. We came in a taxi.

MRS. BURNS. Where is your shoe and stocking?

MARY. I don't know.

MRS. BURNS. What's this? *(Sees edge of stocking peeping out of Doc's handkerchief pocket and pulls it out)* Let us go into our cabin and put it on.

DOC. I think I'd better bandage up the ankle first. *(They go in stateroom Number Three as CHUB comes around deck R.U. MRS. BURNS first. MARY and DOC follow.)* That was a hurried job before. May I come in? *(DOC starts in.)*

MARY. Yes, we will have more privacy in there. *(Looks at CHUB.)*

CHUB. Maybe I can help you. *(DOC hesitates. DOC slams door in CHUB's face.)*

CHUB. Nerve! *(Pulls himself together as G. P. comes around deck R.U., followed by STEWARD with more flowers and a basket of fruit.)*

G. P. Come on—the coast's clear.

STEWARD. *(Stands with back to CHUB, who takes a piece of fruit and puts it in his pocket.)*

STEWARD. Will you open the door for me, sir? Both my hands are full.

G. P. *(Does so)* You want more waiting on than any prima donna I ever saw. (STEWARD *exits into bridal suite.)*

CHUB. *(Looking at door of bridal suite)* Looks like a big night, doesn't it?

G. P. Yes, indeed—we're preparing a little surprise for the bride and groom.

CHUB. Well, I certainly wish them peace and happiness.

G. P. That's very nice of you, young man.

CHUB. You're giving them a good start.

G. P. I suppose you're going to Bermuda.

CHUB. No—I just came to say goodbye to a very particular friend of mine—young lady.

G. P. Young lady? Well, if you'd care to introduce me, I'll look after her on the way down—and by the way, that's the reason why I'm here myself —lady.

CHUB. *(Nudges* G. P. *and they both laugh)* Lady!—I'll bet this is going to be some trip.

G. P. I'll take half your bet.

CHUB. You know at first I thought you were the bridegroom.

G. P. Not yet.

CHUB. But soon?

G. P. I hope. By the way, didn't I see you talking to my niece just now?

CHUB. *(Shaking* G. P.'s *hand cordially)* Is she your niece? Well—well—I'm glad to meet you, sir. I certainly would like to take this trip. The truth is, I can't spare the time right now. I'm very much interested in the market.

G. P. Is that so? I'm slightly interested myself. Have a cigar?

CHUB. *(Taking cigar and waxing important under* G. P.'s *friendship)* Thanks.

G. P. Shall we take a little stroll around the deck?

CHUB. With pleasure.

G. P. How are conditions in the Street right now?

CHUB. Well, now, I'll tell you my idea of the present situation. Now, I've made an exhaustive study. *(Starts to exit. Takes G. P.'s arm in friendly fashion. As they go off R.I STOKES bumps into them with wheelchair. He is surprised at seeing CHUB and G. P. together.)*

STOKES. I beg your pardon.

CHUB. *(Ignoring him)* Please be careful where you are going, young man. *(Walks pompously off with G. P.)*

G. P. *(In passing)* That chair will get you into trouble yet, young man, rolling you around the deck like that.

STOKES. You big stiff! *(As he says this he is turning away from CHUB and is glancing toward bridal suite. STEWARD, who has just entered, thinks he is addressing him.)*

STEWARD. *(With indignation)* I beg your pardon. Were you speaking to me?

STOKES. Is your name Stiff?

STEWARD. No, sir. Smith.

STOKES. Smith! That isn't a name. It's an epidemic.

STEWARD. Epidemic? Oh, no, sir. There is nothing like that the matter with me. My name is Smith, not Stiff.

STOKES. Is the decoration appropriate?

STEWARD. *(Standing by door of bridal suite)* Decoration? I think so, sir. Just step inside and see. I didn't know you belonged to the bridal party. Best man, I presume?

STOKES. No, I'm the bride. Go to the devil. *(Wheels chair to Number Three.)*

STEWARD. *(Starting off)* I never saw such a

touchy bridal party—you'd think they all committed some crime. *(Exits* R.I.)

STOKES. *(Knocking at door)* I have the chair here.

DOC. *(Opens door)* What is it?

STOKES. *(Surprised)* What? You here? Say—this is going a little bit too far, old man.

DOC. What do you mean? Her aunt is there.

STOKES. Oh!

DOC. Besides, I was rendering professional services.

STOKES. That's a great alibi—that professional stuff.

DOC. Gee, I'm glad you knocked on the door just then. Mary is telling her aunt about the invitation. I—I—don't feel well.

STOKES. I have news that will make you happy. Who do you suppose I saw talking to your uncle just now?

DOC. Who?

STOKES. Chub.

DOC. Chub! How did he meet G. P.?

STOKES. Search me. They just went around the deck arm in arm, like a couple of college chums. *(They go up and look off* R.U.)

DOC. Oh, he'll spill the beans as sure as you're alive. *(Down* C.L.)

STOKES. I don't think he knows who G. P. is. It's a cinch G. P. doesn't know who he is, because he was taking Chub seriously.

DOC. What do you suppose G. P. will do when he finds out?

STOKES. Well, the worst he can do is to put us in irons.

CHUB. *(Enter* CHUB *and* G. P., R.U. *They are very confidential and* G. P. *is listening earnestly to* CHUB. CHUB *is smoking his cigar luxuriously)* And

Morgan says to me, "Probably you're right, young man," and that's the way I saved the situation.

G. P. That's a very good idea. (Doc *and* STOKES *exchange glances.*) I'll take the matter up with you when I return. Where can I reach you—care of Morgan?

CHUB. Yes, by the time you get back I guess that will be all right.

STOKES. Oh, Chub—just a minute—Chub! (CHUB *glances at him, undecided whether to recognize him or not.* STOKES *speaks sternly)* Come here! (CHUB *yields.*)

Doc. *(To* G. P.) May I see you alone, sir?

G. P. *(To* CHUB, *very deferentially)* You'll excuse me?

CHUB. *(Up and down* L.) Certainly.

G. P. *(To* Doc) Have you seen the decorations? *(Indicating bridal suite.)*

Doc. No.

G. P. Shall we step in here and talk?

Doc. If you like.

G. P. *(Just before entering)* Wasn't it lucky I could get the bridal suite?

Doc. Yes, indeed!

G. P. I fixed everything fine for you, didn't I?

Doc. You certainly did. You fixed things great. (Doc *and* G. P. *exit into bridal suite.)*

STOKES. *(Fiercely)* Come on, now. What have you been telling him? *(Seizes* CHUB *by arm.)*

CHUB. *(Still trying to be superior; wrenches his arm free and brushes sleeve)* Really, Stokes, you mustn't be so familiar, when I'm talking to people of prominence. That's a very important man.

STOKES. You bet your life he's an important man.

CHUB. Well, don't interrupt me when I'm talking to people like that.

STOKES. No? I'll interrupt your useless life if

you have told him or anybody else on this ship anything about the invitations.

CHUB. (Pathetically) Say, Stokes—this is no way to talk to a pal. Just because those wedding presents were a trifle—disappointing, you and Doc treat me as if I had the smallpox.

STOKES. Well, you do as I say or you'll wish you had the smallpox before the day is over.

CHUB. (Starts R.) All right—I'm through—our friendship ends right here.

STOKES. (Delighted) You promise me that?

CHUB. I wouldn't speak to you again if you were the last man living. Goodbye.

STOKES. Goodbye! (CHUB turns abruptly to go R. just as the door of stateroom Number Three opens and MRS. BURNS looks out.)

MRS. BURNS. Have you the wheelchair for my niece?

CHUB. Yes, Mrs. Burns.

MRS. BURNS. That's splendid—it's just in time.

MARY. (From inside) Oh, Mr. Merchant-Chief —will you introduce my attorney to my Aunt?

MRS. BURNS. (R. of door) Yes, do.

CHUB. (Forgetting his quarrel with STOKES) With pleasure. Mrs. Burns, this is my very dear friend, Mr. Stokes.

MRS. BURNS. How do you do, Mr. Stokes?

STOKES. (Crossing to her) I've met you before on Tag Day.

MRS. BURNS. You, too? I seem to have met all Greater New York on Tag Day.

STOKES. I didn't think you were the aunt.

MRS. BURNS. Why not?

STOKES. One always thinks of a pretty girl's aunt as a severe, spectacled old lady who scares away all men—but you—— Well, me for Auntie! (MRS. BURNS is L. of stateroom Number Three. STOKES stands close to her. CHUB is L. of him.)

CHUB. Here, Stokes—don't be rude.

MRS. BURNS. Rude? I think that's a very pretty compliment.

CHUB. But he's not respectful.

MRS. BURNS. It's very consoling to a woman of my age to have a young man disrespectful, but not rude.

STOKES. Thanks! You look like you'd understand a fellow.

CHUB. *(To* MARY, *as she appears at door)* Shall I help you?

STOKES. Let me help you. *(They help her out.)*

MRS. BURNS. Be careful, dear.

MARY. You know it really isn't painful at all—except when I put my weight on it. *(Sits in chair.)*

MRS. BURNS. Will you young men wheel my niece around the deck? *(STOKES goes to handle of wheelchair. They exit* R.I *ad libbing.* G. P. *and* DOC *come out of bridal suite as* STEWARD *enters* R.I *with more flowers.)*

STEWARD. *(When* DOC *and* G. P. *open door)* Can I get in here?

G. P. Yes, I guess we must vacate and give this soprano a chance. *(STEWARD exits bridal suite.* MRS. BURNS *enters* R.I *and goes in Number Three.)* Look, my boy. Who is that lady going into the stateroom?

DOC. That's Mary's aunt.

G. P. It is? And I didn't recognize her! *(Goes up stage. Starts for her room and hesitates)* She'll be offended at me for not remembering.

DOC. But Uncle, I have something to explain.

G. P. Not now, my boy—not now. Can't you see I'm too excited to listen to anything now?

DOC. *(Enthusiastically)* Then when the ship sails I'll tell you everything. *(MRS. BURNS enters from her stateroom.)*

G. P. Call her. Hurry—she's walking away.

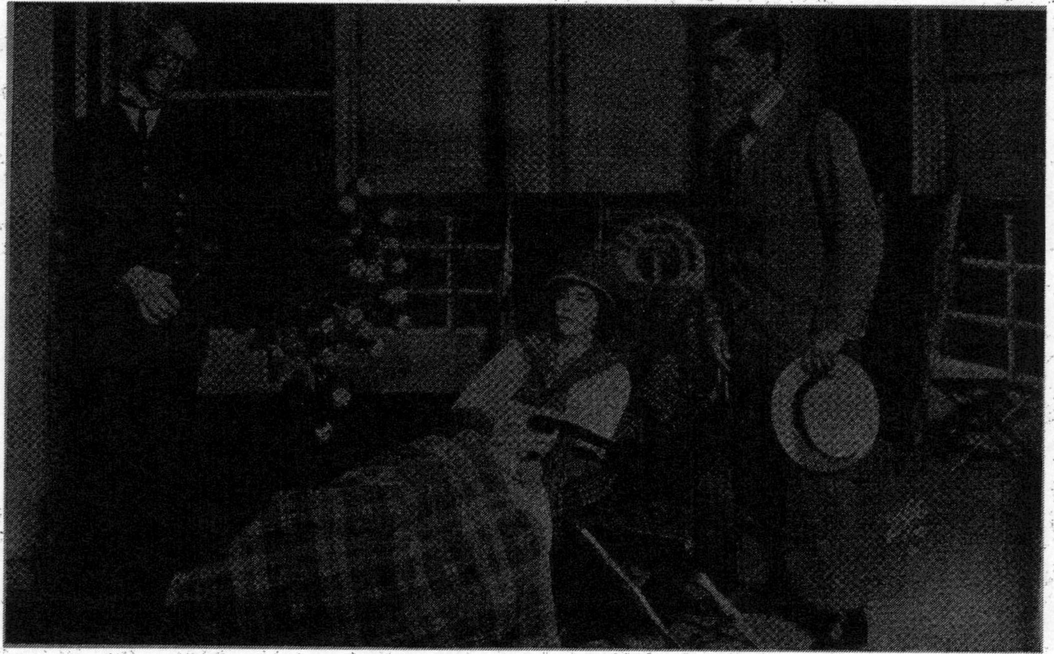

ACT III

*See page* 106

*(Walks up stage; smoothes hair and arranges tie, etc.)*

Doc. *(Calls out)* Mrs. Burns—Mrs. Burns! Just a moment, please.

G. P. *(Coming down stage so* Mrs. Burns *can see him)* Mary!

Mrs. Burns. George! *(They stand looking at each other a moment in silence.* Doc *looks from one to the other.)*

Doc. I think I can ask for my passports now. *(Exits R.I.)*

Mrs. Burns. And to think, George—you didn't even know me! *(Going to steamer-chair; sits on arm.)*

G. P. *(Uncomfortable)* But Mary—I had no idea you would grow so much more beautiful.

Mrs. Burns. *(Laughs)* That pretty speech makes up for it in a measure, although I am disappointed.

G. P. *(Fearfully, thinking of his waist measure)* Really, Mary? I was *afraid* of that. But after twenty years of loneliness—*I'm* satisfied if you'll just tolerate me. *(*Steward *enters* R.I; *laughs and exits* R.I.) There are more funny noises on this ship—— *(Laughs. Comes close to her.)*

Mrs. Burns. Remember we're on deck.

G. P. No, we're not. I'm very close to Paradise. *(WHISTLE blows violently)* Confound that!

Mrs. Burns. You see we are on deck. They don't have whistles in Paradise.

Chub. *(Enters* R.U.) Excuse me.

G. P. *(Looking at* Chub) No; nor rude young intruders.

Chub. I just wanted to say goodbye, sir.

G. P. Goodbye, young man; goodbye.

Chub. *(To* Mrs. Burns) I hope to see you when you get back. You and your niece. (G. P. *looks at* Chub *disapprovingly.)* Goodbye, Mrs. Burns.

G. P. Mrs. Burns, that's right. Somehow, I never

can think of you as Mrs. Burns. You'll always be Mary Jane Smith to me.

CHUB. What?

G. P. Look here, young man, I'm speaking to the lady.

CHUB. Did you say Mary Jane Smith?

G. P. Get out!

CHUB. *(As he crosses to* MRS. BURNS*)* Pardon me, but where do you live?

MRS. BURNS. In Elizabeth, New Jersey.

CHUB. *(As he goes out)* In Elizabeth! Oh, Doc —Doc! (CHUB *backs into wall and stumbles out* R.U. *in confusion.* G. P. *and* MRS. BURNS *follow to rail upstage and look after him.)*

MRS. BURNS. *(Smiling)* Queer little fellow, isn't he?

G. P. He's an impertinent bounder! Just because I spoke to him a few minutes ago, he presumes entirely too much. *(Up* C.)

MRS. BURNS. There's *your* nephew and *my* niece.

G. P. Our nephew and niece.

MRS. BURNS. *(Charmingly)* That young man isn't the only one who presumes.

G. P. She's my niece by marriage.

MRS. BURNS. Supreme presumption! *(Down* L.)

G. P. Well, we'll go into that later. How about a stroll around the deck?

MRS. BURNS. All right. I'll get my coat. I'll be out in a moment. *(She starts across deck and exits Number Three.)*

Doc. *(Rushes on from* R.U. *to* G. P.) Do you remember, I asked you to do something for me and you promised you would?

G. P. Yes.

Doc. Well, will you do it now?

G. P. Certainly I'll do it now. (CHUB, MARY *and* STOKES *enter* R.U.)

MARY. *(To* CHUB*)* Will you take this chair

away? I don't like it. It's too much like an invalid. (CHUB *exits* R.U. *with wheelchair.* MARY *sits in steamer-chair.*)

G. P. Mary, I've been talking to this young chap and I think if you'll wait until the boat sails we can fix things up.

Doc. You see—he understands.

MARY. *(Is puzzled)* Oh! You've told him.

G. P. I know how to make you all happy. I'll give you your wedding present. (MARY *is startled.* Doc *and* STOKES *show renewed interest in life.*) I think you and Mary would rather have a check than some useless ornament. Am I right? *(Takes out check-book and fountain-pen.)*

Doc. Uncle, you are right—write—— Isn't he, Mary?

MARY. Oh, yes, *Uncle* is right.

G. P. But as I believe in the wife handling the bank account, I'll make it out to Mary. (Doc *and* STOKES *almost collapse.* MARY *is amused and laughs at* Doc.)

MARY. I can't accept this. Listen——

G. P. *(Blustering)* Not a word now. Take it to please me. (Doc *tries to get check, but* MARY *snatches it away.*) And would you like to see the bridal suite now? *(Crosses* R.)

MARY. I? I can't walk.

G. P. Then get loving young hubby to carry you. Lucky dog! *(Goes into bridal suite.)*

MARY. You haven't told him?

Doc. I can't seem to lead up to it, somehow. I think I'd better write him a letter.

MARY. Don't talk to me at all. *(Picks up book and starts to read.* CHUB *enters* R.U.)

STOKES. *(Looks at watch)* Five minutes more and we are safe. *(Goes to* Doc.)

Doc. We're safe now, if we can trust this dyna-sorous for five minutes.

CHUB. Don't worry about me. If you had as many brains in your head as I have——

Doc. Your head was the inspiration for the Thermos bottle—a perfect vacuum.

*(GONG rings.)*

STEWARD. *(Enters R.1; exits R.U.)* All ashore—last call—all ashore! *(GONG rings.)*

DOC *and* STOKES. Do you hear that? (Doc *and* STOKES *rush to* CHUB *with one accord.)*

Doc. Why don't you get off the ship?

CHUB. Why don't you get off yourself?

STOKES. Because, Cutie, we're going to Bermuda.

CHUB. That's funny! Bermuda! You two couldn't take a trip to Hoboken.

Doc. Ah—but we don't like Hoboken—we like Bermuda. (G. P. *steps out of bridal suite.)*

STOKES. Yes, the doctor and myself are going to Bermuda.

G. P. *(To* STOKES*)* Oh, are you coming along, too?

STOKES. Why, yes, didn't you know?

G. P. No.

Doc. Yes, indeed. I've induced my attorney to come along also.

G. P. Is that so?

CHUB. *(Sarcastically)* You've induced——

Doc. *(Ignoring* CHUB *and speaking to* G. P.*)* Isn't that splendid?

G. P. Yes—it's all right—if he can spare the time.

CHUB. Ha ha!

G. P. *(Thoroughly annoyed)* Say, what is the matter with that Wall Street young fellow?

STOKES. And, as I was changing my rooms anyway—this seemed the best under the circumstances.

G. P. That's right. It will do you good. Great place, Bermuda!

STOKES. Oh, yes, I've heard of its beauties!

(CLEM *enters* R.U., *unobserved. She has a telegram in one hand and pawn-ticket in the other*) The wonderful corals, the lillies——

CLEM. Yes, and the onions. (BOYS *move.*) Here they are, Maw! Yes! You'd better sneak.

MRS. MERRIVALE. (*Enters* R.U. *To* DOC) You viper that I've nourished in my bosom.

DOC. (*Coming down* C. *between* CLEM *and* MARY. BOYS *are upstage and* G. P. *is* L. *of steamer-chair*) How did you find out where we were?

CLEM. I found this telegram on the desk.

DOC. You find lots of things on my desk. Did you come down purposely to see me off?

CLEM. Purposely.

DOC. How sweet of you, Clementine.

CLEM. Yes, wasn't it? I come to see you off, all right—off the ship and sent to jail.

CHUB. Jail!

CLEM. I'm glad you're here. You were a witness. (*Pointing to* CHUB, *who backs upstage.*)

DOC. I don't understand.

CLEM. No? Well, maybe you can understand this. (*Points to pawn-ticket.*)

G. P. What is it?

DOC. A little matter I forgot.

MRS. MERRIVALE. Forgot! I hate to be hard on a doctor whose medicine I've enjoyed so much, but you knew perfectly well I'd need some money for Pollyanna—three dollars and ninety cents and five dollars for her board.

MARY. Her board? That's dreadful!

G. P. What have you been doing, young man—trifling?

CLEM. I should say he has.

MARY. Paying her board!

DOC. No, I haven't been paying anything.

G. P. Do you owe this money?

DOC. Yes, sir, I do.

G. P. What—and you admit it right in front of your wife?

MRS. MERRIVALE. His wife! I thought he was a gentleman—not a married man.

CHUB. *(Starts* R.*)* He is not!

STOKES. *(Pulling* CHUB *back)* Keep still, you idiot.

G. P. Did he tell you he wasn't married?

CLEM. Did he? Why, only this afternoon he gave me his word of honor he wasn't married.

G. P. What's this?

MRS. MERRIVALE. *(She is almost in tears and deliberately creates the impression it was a love affair)* He promised me faithfully he wouldn't leave me.

G. P. The mother, too? This is beyond belief.

MARY. Mother! Daughter! Pollyanna is probably the grandchild.

MRS. MERRIVALE. It's a serpent I've nourished in my bosom.

MARY. I'm glad I found out in time.

CLEM. This young man heard him.

CHUB. Let me explain.

STOKES. *(Pulls him back)* Keep out of this, you idiot.

G. P. *(To* DOC*)* If there is anything between you and this young woman——

MRS. MERRIVALE. *(Crosses to him)* You horrid old man! What are you tryin' to do—make my innocent little girl a correspondent? *(Puts her arm around* CLEM *and in patting her, keeps pushing her hat to one side.* CLEM *protests vigorously and finally pushes her mother's arm away.)*

MARY. Of course—it's nothing to me.

G. P. Nothing to you—— It should be everything to you.

MARY. However, I do think—under the circumstances—an explanation is due. (CLEM *is* R., *then* MRS. MERRIVALE. DOC *is next to* MARY *in steamer-*

*chair.* G. P. *at* L. *of chair.* CHUB *and* STOKES *up* L.)

G. P. It certainly is.

Doc. If you just give me a chance, I can explain everything.

MARY. Yes, give him a chance and he can explain anything.

MRS. MERRIVALE. And to think that I trusted him so.

CHUB. *(Crosses to* G. P. STOKES *follows)* I think I can clear things up. He isn't married—I assure you.

G. P. You don't know what you're talking about.

CHUB. I give you my word of honor he isn't married. (STOKE *tries in vain to shut up* CHUB.)

G. P. Don't be a damned fool—he is married.

CHUB. I tell you he isn't.

G. P. How do you know? He isn't married to you.

CHUB. How do you know, he isn't married to you either?

G. P. I'm his uncle—I ought to know.

CHUB. Oh, my God! *(Backs up* L. *with* STOKES.)

STOKES. *(Softly)* Now are you satisfied?

CHUB. How was I to know?

MARY. And now, if it isn't asking too much, will you be good enough to explain your relations with these ladies? (MRS. MERRIVALE *gives a little scream.*)

Doc. I promised this lady I would not leave her because she became unstrung when she realized she would be deprived of my professional services—so to protect Mrs. Merrivale's health I told her I was not married.

CHUB. I can vouch for that.

G. P. I wouldn't believe *you.*

MRS. MERRIVALE. Was it really to protect my health? *(Placing her hand fondly on* Doc's *arm. He takes it off.)*

Doc. Yes—we professional men must occasionally stretch the truth.

Mary. Yes, I've noticed that.

G. P. Is this true?

Doc. I leave it to the ladies themselves.

Clem. But that doesn't excuse your leaving Pollyanna.

Mary. Yes, what about Pollyanna?      ,

Doc. Pollyanna is a pet parrot.

Mary. A parrot—— You can scarcely expect us to believe that you have been paying a parrot's board.

Doc. Clementine—is Pollyanna a parrot?

Clem. Swears like one.

Doc. Mrs. Merrivale thought her parrot was sick.

Mr. Merrivale. She was sick. We were *both* sick.

Clem. Yes, and she foolishly took it to him and he pawned it.

Stokes. I feel I must rise in defense of my client—he did not pawn the parrot.

Clem. He did too! Here's the pawn-ticket!

Stokes. This gentleman—*(Points to* Chub*)*—pawned the parrot.

Chub. *(Startled and disgusted with* Stokes*)* Oh—come now. *(Exits* r.u. *with* Stokes.*)*

Clem. I never did like his looks.

Mrs. Merrivale. Neither did I—but I thought he looked that way because he was sick.

Doc. However, I will pay for his indiscretion. How much is it?

Clem. Three dollars and ninety cents and five dollars—whatever that comes to.

Doc. *(Feeling in pockets)* Dear me—I didn't have a chance to go to the bank. Clem *grunts.)*

G. P. How much do you need?

Doc. How much is it?

G. P. Here—here's ten dollars.

Doc. *(Crosses to her)* Here, Clementine, is ten dollars.

Clem. I ain't got no change.

Doc. You may keep the change. And now, Clementine, before you go, will you assure this—*(Looks first at* Mary, *then at* Group*)* —party—that you have no claim on me whatsoever?

Clem. Claim! She's welcome to you—*believe me!*

Mary. You're too kind.

Clem. Tastes differ! Now that you've given up your rooms, what will I do with your things?

Doc. You mean those silk-what-do-you-call-'em? You can have those, Clementine.

Clem. How dare you! I am a decent girl. *(Starts to go. WHISTLE blows.)*

Mrs. Merrivale. I don't see anything wrong in silk lingerie.

Clem. All right, then—you wear 'em.

Steward. *(Entering* r.u.*)* All ashore—all ashore—— Are you making the trip, young lady?

Clem. Not with that bunch! (Clem *exits* r.i.)

Steward. *(To* Mrs. Merrivale*)* May I help you off the boat, madam?

Mrs. Merrivale. The Admiral, I suppose? *(She is very coquettish with him.)*

Steward. *(Laughs foolishly)* What's the matter with you? You don't look so well.

Mrs. Merrivale. Oh, Captain, I'm very frail—heart trouble, lungs affected, hardly any stomach, and Captain, you ought to see my poor liver.

Steward. I'll look you up the next time I come to New York. (Both *exit* r.i., *laughing foolishly at each other.)*

Doc. Did I explain everything to your satisfaction?

G. P. *(Crosses to* Doc*)* I admit, for a moment she had me worried. Of course, I knew in my heart

that you wouldn't do anything underhanded——
That's one thing about him, Mary—he's above board
—he inherits that. If there's one thing I cannot tolerate—it's deception.

MARY. How can you stand there and listen to
that?

DOC. Yes, I think I'd better go. (MRS. BURNS
*enters from Number Three.*)

G. P. *(Seeing her)* Excuse me. Ready for our
walk, Mary?

MRS. BURNS. Yes, George. *(They go off R.U.)*

MARY. You're a brute. *(Enter STEWARD R.U. with
huge bouquet of flowers. Doc goes to L. of steamer-
chair.)*

STEWARD. With the Captain's compliments—for
the bride.

MARY. *(Furiously, to Doc)* There you are.

Doc. I think that's very charming of the Captain.

MARY. You do? Well, you take them—*(Throws
bouquet on deck at Doc's feet. To STEWARD)* —and
you tell the Captain I don't want his compliments.

STEWARD. *(To Doc)* Squally weather so soon,
sir? (STEWARD *starts to exit R.I.*)

MARY. Call him back, please.

Doc. Steward.

STEWARD. Yes, sir.

Doc. The lady wants to speak to you.

STEWARD. *(To her)* Your husband says you
wish to speak to me.

MARY. My husband! Who told you I was married?

STEWARD. Everybody on the boat knows it by
now.

MARY. *(Definitely)* I'm not married, I tell you.

STEWARD. Not married—— *(Looks significantly
at bridal suite)* Are you sure?

MARY. Did you ever hear of anything so ridiculous? Must I prove that I'm not married? What

right have you to accuse me of such a thing? I'm not married and that settles it.

STEWARD. I'm sorry you told me that, Miss.

MARY. Why?

STEWARD. I must report it to the Captain.

MARY. That's exactly what I want you to do.

STEWARD. I'm afraid there will be some trouble about the room.

MARY. Why should there be any trouble about the room?

STEWARD. *(Embarrassed)* Well—ma'm—they're very strict about that sort of thing on this line. *(Exits* R.I. *Ad lib. "I do wish you hadn't told me.")*

MARY. *(In a temper. Realizing what he means)* Oh! How dare you insult me like that? Are you going to stand by and allow him to say such things to me? *(She starts to cry.)*

Doc. *(Goes to chair and puts arm around* MARY's *shoulder)* Why, Mary, you're crying. Please don't cry—I can't stand that.

MARY. You've compromised me dreadfully.

Doc. I wouldn't do that for the world.

MARY. But you have done it. *(Doc reaches for his handkerchief and pulls out her stocking. She throws it on the deck; cries again.)*

Doc. *(Crossing* R.) Well, I'll go—I'll leave the ship.

MARY. And have everyone say—you deserted me? I should say not.

Doc. What do you want me to do, then?

MARY. Tell them we're not married. *(Enter* STOKES R.I.*)*

Doc. Why did you desert me just now?

STOKES. I thought I had better go and give you a clear field.

Doc. Don't mix your metaphors, Stokes. We are on a ship and if you want to clear anything—clear the decks for action.

CHUB. *(Entering* R.I) Hey! Fellows! There's an awful scandal on board. I just heard the Steward talking to the Captain. It seems two fellows and a girl have the bridal suite and they're not married. (MARY *screams.)* The Captain said something about putting them in irons. What do you say? Let's stick around and see what comes off.

MARY. *(Exasperated and in tears)* Oh! Oh! Are you going to tell him now or are you not?

DOC. *(Starts up)* I am going now.

STOKES. Now. *(Looks at watch)* You don't mean exactly now—— (STOKES *is* C. CHUB *is* R. *of* STOKES. DOC *is* R. *of* MARY.)

DOC. Mary says now, but before I go—I swear to you, Mary Jane Smith——

CHUB. *(To him)* Doc—you're all wrong. This isn't Mary Jane Smith——

DOC. Chub—you don't want to see me tried for murder, do you?

CHUB. No.

DOC. Then keep away from me, that's all.

MARY. I'll scream if you don't go.

DOC. I'm going. *(He exits* R.U. STOKES, *looking at watch and hoping to kill time until the boat sails.)*

CHUB. *(To* STOKES*)* But Stokes—you don't understand—the aunt is Mary Jane Smith.

MARY. I am Mary Jane Smith!

CHUB. What?

MARY. And I know about the invitations and whose name was used and whose idea it was, and I wouldn't have too much to say if I were you.

CHUB. I—I—— *(Looks from one to the other)* I—I——

STOKES. For the first time in his life he's speechless. *(NOISE of argument off* R.U. *Enter,* R.U., DOC, *running at full speed. G. P. can be heard off stage; is very angry.)*

DOC. I told him.

STOKES. What is he going to do?

Doc. I think he's going to sink the ship.

CHUB. Did he say anything?

Doc. Plenty—he's saying it yet.

G. P. (*Enters* R.U., *followed by* MRS. BURNS, *who goes to* MARY) You infernal scoundrel! (*LIGHTS slowly dim. First border out. Foots two-thirds down. Back border down and out.*) I'll disown you—that's what I'll do. (*Goes to where the* THREE BOYS *are.*)

Doc. Uncle—please—not here.

G. P. Yes—right here—now—I'll expose you for the unprincipled dog that you are. Make a fool of me, will you? You and your unscrupulous friends! (CHUB *and* STOKES *back against cabin wall on words* "*unscrupulous friends.*")

Doc. (*To him*). Not so loud. I'm going.

G. P. Get off the ship before I throw you off.

CHUB. (*Coming to* G. P.) Just a minute, sir. It's really my fault.

G. P. Then I'll throw you off too. (CHUB *backs away, frightened.*)

STOKES. (*To* G. P.) We're all equally to blame.

G. P. (*Grabbing* STOKES *by the collar and shaking him*) Oh! You're getting noble about it now. You're all crooks and I'll have you put in jail—the whole nasty crew of you.

Doc. (*To* G. P.) Please don't cause a scene like this, sir. (MRS. BURNS *enters the group. She has been talking to* MARY *and they have apparently arrived at an understanding.*)

G. P. And why should I show you any consideration?

Doc. I'm thinking of the ladies.

G. P. So am I. You've insulted the niece of the woman I'm going to marry——

MRS. BURNS. (*To him*) Just a minute, George.

I think you take things just a bit too much for granted.

G. P. In what way?

MRS. BURNS. I'm not so sure I'm going to marry you.

G. P. Mary—please don't say that. You can't blame me for what my nephew has done.

MRS. BURNS. No—but I can blame you for what you are doing to your nephew. If you can't control your temper in a case of this kind——

G. P. But do you realize what he has done? But you can't. Why, he sent out wedding invitations and used Mary's name.

MARY. But he didn't *know* it was my name.

DOC. *(To her)* You're wonderful—I didn't know anyone could be such a brick.

MRS. BURNS. If he hadn't been so close with you in money matters you wouldn't have had to do it, would you?

DOC. No—I was desperate for money. Wasn't I, boys?

STOKES *and* CHUB. *(With exaggerated sympathy)* I should say you were. Didn't have a nickel—— *(Ad lib.)*

MARY. *(To* G. P.*)* He was almost starving, while you were living in the lap of luxury.

MRS. BURNS. The poor boy! *(Putting hand on* Doc's *shoulder.* MARY *and* MRS. BURNS *look sympathetically at* DOC. STOKES *and* CHUB *place hands on* DOC. G. P. *is completely nonplussed and keeps twirling his hat nervously.)*

G. P. Well, of course, I had no idea he was as hard up as that. Why, dog-gone it, you all make me feel that I'm the culprit and he's the hero. You seem to see things different than I do. I guess I'm all out of focus. I won't make the trip. I'll go back where I belong. *(Starts to move.)*

MRS. BURNS. George! How little you have

changed. It was the same when you left me twenty
years ago.

G. P. *(To her)* You can't think much of me. If
you are going to let that scamp come between us.

MRS. BURNS. That's just what I was thinking.
*(Goes back to MARY's side.)*

Doc. Uncle George, don't, please don't let my
ridiculous escapade spoil your romance. It *was* a
preposterous scheme.

G. P. Then you admit it was preposterous!

Doc. Yes, sir. I didn't realize just how preposterous until I received Aunt Jane's present.

G. P. *(Smiles in spite of himself)* What was
that? A nightie—wasn't it?

Doc. Yes, sir—a nightie—for the bride.

G. P. That was funny. *(Laughs)* And Aunt
Margaret sent a handsome kimona. Ha! Ha!

Doc. Also for the bride!

MRS. BURNS. I didn't hear about that.

G. P. Kimonas and lingerie and all sorts of
pretties—for the bride.

Doc. Nothing for the groom.

G. P. Not a thing!

MARY. Even your check is made out to me.

CHUB. Then you *did* come across?

G. P. Oh, ho—so you were in on that, too?

CHUB. Yes, it was my idea!

G. P. It was, eh? Then why did you allow me
to get two tickets? *(To Doc.)*

Doc. Well—you see—that——

MARY. That was my idea. When you said you
had two tickets, I suggested that our attorney come
along.

G. P. There seems to be a general conspiracy with
me as the financial goat.

*(WHISTLE. LONG BLAST. BELL. The boat
starts, or rather the drop at back starts moving*

*the effect of movement. The back drop is on
a windlass and moves along, giving the effect
of ship moving. The scene is the skyline of
New York and then the bay.)*

CHUB. The boat's going! Let me off! I have no
ticket! What will I do?

STOKES. *(Grabbing* CHUB*)* You said we treated
you as if you had the smallpox—so we'll drop you
at Quarantine.

CHUB. I wish you all luck. I'll go and see the
Captain about getting off.

DOC. Where are you going when you do get off,
Chub?

CHUB. Search me.

G. P. You broke, too?

CHUB. Oh, I'll get along—all right——

G. P. I thought you were interested in Wall
Street?

CHUB. I was, sir—interested.

DOC. In a futuristic way.

G. P. I see—— Well, I tell you, young man—
perhaps I can use you as my secretary. Anybody
with your ideas might be valuable.

CHUB. *(Crosses to him)* You mean that, sir?

G. P. I don't bluff.

DOC. I know who I have to thank for this.
You're the most wonderful, the sweetest, finest——
*(To* MRS. BURNS.*)*

STOKES. *(To* AUNTIE*)* You know what I said—
"Me for Auntie." Isn't she a wonder? *(Takes* MRS.
BURNS' *arm.)*

G. P. That will do. I've forgiven you boys once.
Don't start anything more. *(Crossing to rail of
steamer with* MRS. BURNS. *LIGHTS dim down to
Blues. SPOTS on.)*

DOC. Boys, there's a lovely view right around the
deck.

CHUB. I like the view here.

STOKES. O.K. Come on—Chub. *(Exits R.I. Doc gets steamer-chair from rail and places it at MARY's R. The chairs are close together.)*

MRS. BURNS. I think the sky line of New York from the deck of a steamer is the most beautiful sight in the world.

G. P. You do? That's because you can't see what I see!

MRS. BURNS. How sweet of you. *(G. P. takes her hand and they exit R.U.)*

DOC. He ought to see what I see.

MARY. You mean my ankle? *(WARN Curtain.)*

DOC. No, I mean Mary Jane Smith.

MARY. That is an awful name when you think of it.

DOC. It certainly is. I'd change it if I were you. By the way, where is that check Uncle gave you?

MARY. I have it right here—why?

DOC. I was just thinking you can't cash that unless you marry me.

MARY. Who said I wanted to cash it?

DOC. What is the check for?

MARY. For a wedding present.

DOC. No—I mean—what's the amount?

MARY. It's for ten thousand dollars.

DOC. *(Sitting up quickly)* Ten thousand dollars! Mary, listen to reason. *(Doc takes out stateroom tickets)* Here I am with a bridal suite and no bride? Won't you take this?

MARY. What?

DOC. For yourself and your aunt.

MARY. I wouldn't occupy that room for this ten thousand dollars—after all the notoriety I've been subjected to. *(Gives them back to him.)*

DOC. *(After a short pause)* Well, what will I do with this check, Mary—tear it up?

MARY. *(Reaching out her hand and taking check, smiling)* No—no—it's no use tearing it up. *(He reaches over and kisses her.)*

## CURTAIN

## "MARY'S ANKLE"

## PROPERTY PLOT

## ACT I

*Interior Doctor's Office and Living Room*

*On Stage:*

Ground cloth.
Medallion.
Two smaller rugs.
Practical window-shades on windows R. and L.
Cretonne curtains on windows R. and L.
Small table L. above window.
Chair on each side.
Magazines on small table L.
Chaise lounge L. made up as bed—
Two sheets.
Pillow.
Counterpane.
Small stool R. of lounge.
Armchair up L. of closet.
Three sofa pillows in armchair—one to be small
   and lace covered.
Three hooks on closet door up C.
Shelf in closet with hooks underneath and
Clothes hangers in closet.
Cretonne-covered chest in closet.
Suitcase in closet.
Chiffonier R. of closet.
Key in door Center.

*On Chiffonier:*
Two candlesti.cks.
Mirror.
Doilie or cloth.

Cretonne-covered screen R. of chiffonier.
Flat-topped desk down R. with drawers.
Upholstered chair, cretonne-covered, L. of table or
     desk.
Armchair R. of table or desk.

*On the Desk:*
20 Pawn-tickets in drawer of desk.
Three empty beer bottles.
Doctor's medical case.
Chafing dish.
Two Doctor's thermometers in glass.
Matchstand.
Ashtray.
Appointment-book.
Pads.
Desk-blotter.
Pens.
Pencils in brass holder.
Note paper in brass holder.
Big brass letter-opener.
Two pair Doctor's scissors.
Brass calendar-holder.
Washstand and porcelain basin up R. of desk.
Towel-rack above basin.
Two soiled towels on towel-rack.
Doctor's operating table R. of desk.
One pillow for operating table.
One sheet for operating table.
Doctor's operating stool R. of table.
Doctor's cabinet extreme R. filled with bottles of
     different sizes and bandages.

*On top of cabinet:*
Two small medical cases.
Two rolls of bandages.
One roll adhesive plaster.
One bottle smelling-salts.

Doctor's medical stand below cabinet—glass top.
Medical instruments for Doctor's stand.

*In Bathroom, Up Stage Right:*
Set bowl, practical.
Towel-rack above.
Two clean bath-towels on rack.
Glass.
Toothbrush.
Tooth-powder.
Mirror which draws out.
Brush.
Comb.
Pictures on flats in set.
Doctor's diploma.

*Off Stage L.—Act I:*
Parrot on perch or in cage for Mrs. Merrivale.
Cane for Mrs. Merrivale.
Carpet-sweeper for Clem.
Dustpan and feather duster for Clem.
Brush for Clem.
Two clean towels for Clem.
Telephone directory, New York.
Three one-dollar bills, for Chub.
One quarter, for Chub.
One nickel, for Chub.
Six dimes, for Chub.
Cracker for parrot, for Mrs. Merrivale.
Pawn-ticket, for Chub.
Six letters.

Tag Day flags, for Mary.
Bag for Mary.
Newspaper for Chub.

## ACT II

### *Same Set as Act I*

*On Stage:*
Small lace-covered pillow at foot of stool R. of
    lounge.
Screen R. of chiffonier taken over R. and set to cover
    operating table.
Doctor's operating stool and basin and stand—to be
    taken off.
Doctor's medical book down stage end of table—on
    table.
Wedding invitations in two envelopes on table,
    down stage end.
Doctor's medical case up stage end of table on floor.
Piece of iron under rug—so as to break glass vase
    or punch bowl.

*Off Stage:*
Telegram.
Hospital reports.
Pipe.
Tobacco-pouch.
Cigarette-box with one cigarette (Egyptian).
Medical book.
Expressman's book and pencil.
Seven assorted express packages.
*Effect of automobile collision.*
Horns.
Glass crash, etc.
Doorbell.
Grip for G. P.
Wedding invitation for G. P.
Stage money for G. P.

Notebook for Stokes.
7 Express packages—each package to contain one
    of these articles with cards enclosed:
    A beautiful nightdress.
    A Japanese kimona.
    A pair of fancy pajamas.
    A small case of jewels.
    Three pieces of lingerie.
    Glass vase or punch bowl (cut glass) to break.
    Towels and linen.
Small notepad for Doc.
Electric fan back of window L.
Vacuum cleaner.

## ACT III

*Deck of the Steamship Bermudian*

*On Stage:*
Ground cloth.
Two life-preservers on rail of ship.

*In Bridal Suite:*
Brass bed made up.
Chiffonier.
Two pedestal stands in windows R. and L., with glass
    vases to hold flowers.

*In Stateroom Number Three:*
Regular ship's bunk, upper and lower made up (op-
    tional).
Book and box of candy on lower bunk.
Hat tree.
Mirror (optional).

*Off Stage:*
*In R. First Entrance:*
Steamer-chair, with steamer-rug tacked to back.
Steamer-rug on arm of steamer-chair.

*Back of Bridal Suite up* C.:
Rollchair (invalid).
Champagne basket.
Large candy-box.
Six large bouquets.
Two baskets of fruit.
Steamer-chair.
Traveling-bag.
Suitcase.
Dinner-gong for Steward.
Cigars for G. P.
Checkbook for G. P.
Fountain-pen for G. P.
Steamship tickets for G. P.
Telegram for Clem.
Pawn-tickets for Clem.
Cane for Mrs. Merrivale.
Ship's bell.
Boat whistle L. first entrance.
Rainbox.
Magazines for Mrs. Burns.

## "MARY'S ANKLE"

## PUBLICITY THROUGH YOUR LOCAL
## PAPERS

The press can be an immense help in giving publicity to your productions. In the belief that the best reviews from the New York and other large papers are always interesting to local audiences, and in order to assist you, we are printing below several excerpts from those reviews.

To these we have also added a number of suggested press notes which may be used either as they stand or changed to suit your own ideas and submitted to the local press.

"The play is light, frequently gay, and really funny."—*"New York Times."*

"'Mary's Ankle' deals with a completely preposterous idea and many absurd situations, which is the stuff of which all good farces are made. It has novelty of treatment and more than a few hilarious situations."—*"New York World."*

"'Mary's Ankle' arrived briskly in New York last night. It is a farce of youth, financial need and a compound fracture of a honeymoon. It is a play in which many will find real amusement."—*"New York Herald."*

"From 'The Three Musketeers' to 'La Boheme' down to 'Mary's Ankle' the spectacle of three youths in a harum-scarum, helter-skelter, undaunted and generally ineffective struggle with poverty has furnished always delectable scenes. 'Mary's Ankle'

proved to be a bright little farce."—"*New York
Evening Sun.*"

"'Mary's Ankle' perfectly lady-like. Alan Dale
finds amusement, fresh situations and droll dialogue.
We laughed at 'Mary's Ankle' and that is precisely
all we were intended to do."—"*New York American.*"

"New Yorkers had their first view of 'Mary's
Ankle' last night and the humor is the sort usually
described as 'riotous.' The fun was fast and furious and kept the audience in almost constant laughter."—"*New York Journal.*"

"The big virtue of 'Mary's Ankle' lies in the fact
that it is most amusing, full of laughs and a sure
gloom chaser. And what more can a person wish?
The theatre's chief mission, after all, is to entertain.
If it can also educate or preach a moral, so much
the better. But entertainment's the thing."—"*New
York Globe.*"

"The best example of farce given us since 'Seven
Days.'"—"*Atlantic City Gazette-Review.*"

"There is brisk and peppery fun a plenty in
'Mary's Ankle.' Strangely enough, there is not an
immodest situation or an indelicate suggestion in
the whole performance. It is one of the cleanest
and most hilariously amusing plays in recent years."
—"*Boston Globe.*"

"'Mary's Ankle,' a farce, has the sterling merit of
being both vastly amusing and absolutely clean.
There is not even a suspicion of suggestiveness
from start to finish. The characters are all well
drawn and full of comedy touches, the dialogue
fairly sparkles and the situations which come quick
on top of each other are very funny."—"*New York
Review.*"

"May Tully took her place last night with Margaret Mayo and Claire Kummer as a writer of clever
farce. Her play, 'Mary's Ankle,' is altogether amus-

ing and without deadly moments."—"*Boston Journal.*"

" 'Mary's Ankle' supplies the title to a very fresh and airy farce. Contrary to what the title might lead some persons to believe, it is devoid of impropriety, coarseness and double entendre. It is as fresh and wholesome as the East Wind."—"*Boston American.*"

"A bright, clean-cut, laugh-provoking farce. The story is at all times amusing, ingenuous and within the range of possibility."—*Edward Harold Crosby, "Boston Post."*

" 'Mary's Ankle' is an entertaining farce. Despite the feminine authorship—May Tully wrote it—the humor is masculine."—"*Boston Transcript.*"

" 'Twin Beds' was funny. 'Turn To the Right' was, if possible, more so, likewise 'The Boomerang.' And now 'Mary's Ankle.' There is more humor in the latter. It is an exhilaration of laughter."—"*Atlantic City Daily Press.*"

In submitting "Mary's Ankle" for the delectation of the public the —————— Players are thoroughly mindful of the fact that the local theatregoers want their entertainment clean as well as funny. There is not a line nor a situation in this sparkling comedy to which exception can be taken, and yet it will stir your risibilities to the Nth degree. It has been a great favorite throughout the country, both as a touring attraction and in the stock companies. It has at last been released for amateur use owing to the great demand from all over the country, and the —————— Players have made a ten-strike in securing the right to present it here.

So we urge all those who delight in clean, wholesome fun to foregather at the —————— Theatre on —————— evening and revel in an evening of continuous laughter.

## SYNOPSIS

"Mary's Ankle" is the story of ambitious but impecuniary youth. "Doc" Hampton, without a patient, "Stoksie," a lawyer devoid of clients, and "Chub" Perkins, a financier with only schemes for capital, are in a bad way. In fact, they are broke and it is almost a problem of how to obtain food. Only the fact that "Doc's" landlady, Mrs. Merrivale, makes a specialty of having diseases to which he gives his professional attention makes it possible to keep the roof over his head.

Mary Jane Smith is the heroine with the ankle. The three pals meet her first as a solicitor of funds for the poor and again as the victim of an automobile accident.

A rich relative, "Doc's" uncle, inclined to be a tightwad but good at heart, comes into the scene and seeing Mary, immediately takes it for granted that she is his nephew's wife, having been informed by a bogus wedding invitation that the ceremony has just taken place.

It was "Chub's" idea to get the family "back home" in the West to send wedding presents that could be pawned. What do they bring? Nothing but gifts for the bride, and mostly wearing apparel at that.

The injured Mary proves to be the Mary Jane Smith of the wedding announcements, and from then on the farce moves hilariously for the audience and tragically for the boys, especially "Doc," who has "fallen" completely for Mary.

The Uncle has come East after twenty years to meet an old sweetheart, and as his wedding present insists that "Doc" and Mary accompany him to Bermuda. The situation is tense, but Mary has a sense of humor. Mary is a grand old name and this

Mary is a grand girl. She jumps into the breach and saves the day, but not without keeping the boys guessing as to whether or not she will give them away to the now ferocious Uncle.

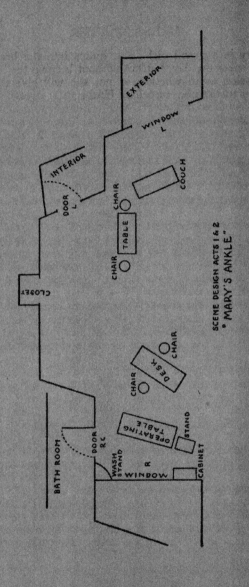

SCENE DESIGN ACTS 1 & 2
"MARY'S ANKLE"

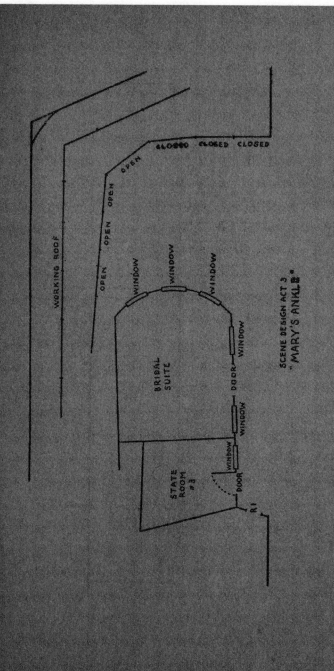

SCENE DESIGN ACT 3
" MARY'S ANKLE "

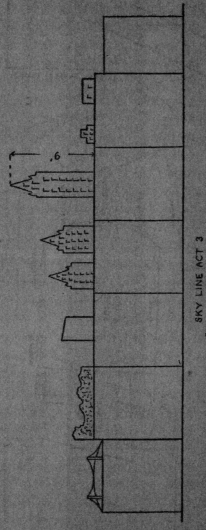

SKY LINE ACT 3
"MARY'S ANKLE"

CPSIA information can be obtained
at www.ICGtesting.com
Printed in the USA
BVHW04*1020220618
519746BV00009B/57/P